Let's Get C

COCKTAILS

Over **100** brilliant drinks

igloobooks

iqloobooks

Published in 2017
by Igloo Books Ltd
Cottage Farm
Sywell
NN6 0BJ
www.igloobooks.com

Designed by Nicholas Gage
Edited by Jasmin Peppiatt

All imagery © iStock / Getty Images

LEO002 0717
2 4 6 8 10 9 7 5 3 1
ISBN 978-1-78670-861-8

Printed and manufactured in China

Contents

Cocktails

SERVES: 1 | PREPARATION TIME: 5 MINS

Tequila Sunrise

6 ice cubes
2 shots tequila
orange juice
1 shot grenadine

TO SERVE
1 cherry
1 orange slice

1. Pour the tequila into a tall glass filled with the ice.
2. Top up with orange juice.
3. Pour the grenadine down the inside of the glass so it sinks to the bottom.
4. Garnish with a cherry and an orange slice.
5. Serve immediately.

SERVES: 1 | PREPARATION TIME: 5 MINS

Mojito

10 mint leaves
1 tsp sugar syrup
1 tsp sugar
1 shot white rum
1 shot lime juice
1 lime, cut into small chunks
5 ice cubes
soda water

1. Mash the mint, sugar syrup and sugar together in a glass or jar, ensuring the mint leaves are crushed to release the flavour.
2. Add the rum, lime juice, lime chunks and ice.
3. Top up with soda water and stir well with a cocktail mixer.
4. Serve immediately with extra ice, if desired.

Orgasm

1 handful ice cubes
2 shots Irish cream liqueur
1 shot amaretto
1 shot coffee liqueur
2 shots cream
4 shots milk

1. Put the ice into the cocktail shaker.
2. Add the Irish cream liqueur, amaretto, coffee liqueur, cream and milk over the ice in the shaker, then shake for 20 seconds.
3. Strain into a glass, adding more ice if desired.

SERVES: **1** | PREPARATION TIME: **5 MINS**

Watermelon Woo Woo

3 ice cubes
1 shot peach schnapps
1 shot vodka
2 shots cranberry juice
4 shots watermelon juice

TO SERVE
1 lime slice
sprig of mint
1 handful crushed ice (optional)

1. Put the ice into the cocktail shaker.
2. Pour the peach schnapps and vodka over the ice in the shaker, then shake for at least 20 seconds.
3. Pour into a glass and top up with the cranberry juice and watermelon juice.
4. Serve immediately, garnished with a slice of lime and a sprig of mint.
5. If desired, top up with crushed ice.

SERVES: **1** | PREPARATION TIME: **5 MINS**

Piña Colada

4 ice cubes
2 shots white rum
5 shots pineapple juice
2 shots coconut cream

TO SERVE
sprig of mint
1 pineapple wedge, peeled
1 vanilla pod

1. Put the ice cubes into the cocktail shaker.
2. Pour the white rum, pineapple juice and coconut cream over the ice in the shaker and shake for 30 seconds.
3. Pour into a tall glass.
4. Serve garnished with a mint sprig, pineapple wedge and vanilla pod.

SERVES: **1** | PREPARATION TIME: **5 MINS**

Black Russian

4 ice cubes
1 shot coffee liqueur
1 shot vodka
cola

TO SERVE
1 lime slice

1. Put the ice into the cocktail shaker.
2. Add the coffee liqueur and vodka over the ice in the shaker, then shake for 10 seconds.
3. Pour into a glass and top up with cola.
4. Serve immediately, garnished with a slice of lime.

Mint Lemon Drop

2 handfuls crushed ice
2 shots vodka
2 shots lemon juice
1 shot lime juice
1 mint sprig
1 tsp sugar syrup
lemonade
1 lemon wedge
1 lime wedge

TO SERVE
1 lime slice

1. Put the crushed ice into the cocktail shaker.
2. Add the vodka, lemon juice and lime juice over the ice in the shaker, then shake for 10 seconds.
3. Crush the mint sprig and add it with the sugar syrup to the glass, then pour in the mixture from the shaker.
4. Top up with lemonade.
5. Run the extra lemon wedge and lime wedge around the edge of the glass for added flavour.
6. Serve immediately, garnished with a lime slice.

SERVES: **1** | PREPARATION TIME: **5 MINS**

Lime Zinger

2 handfuls ice cubes
2 shots lime juice
1 shot lime cordial
1 shot tequila
soda water

TO SERVE
1 lime slice
extra ice cubes

1. Put the ice into the cocktail shaker.
2. Pour the lime juice, lime cordial and tequila over the ice in the cocktail shaker, then shake for 10 seconds.
3. Strain the mixture into the glass, topping it up with soda water.
4. Serve garnished with a lime slice and extra ice cubes.

Mint Ginfusion

2 handfuls ice cubes
2 shots lime juice
½ shot lime cordial
½ tsp sugar syrup
1 tsp mint syrup
5 mint leaves
2 shots gin
soda water

TO SERVE
1 handful blueberries
sprig of mint

1. Put the ice into the cocktail shaker.
2. Put the lime juice, lime cordial, sugar syrup, mint syrup, mint leaves and gin in the cocktail shaker, then shake for 20 seconds, aiming to crush the mint leaves to release flavour.
3. Strain the mixture into the glass, topping it up with soda water.
4. Serve garnished with a handful of blueberries and sprig of mint.
5. If desired, thread some blueberries onto a cocktail stick and rest it in the glass for added decoration.

SERVES: 1 | PREPARATION TIME: 5 MINS

Bloody Mary

4 ice cubes
2 dashes Worcestershire sauce
1 dash hot sauce
1 shot vodka
1 dash lemon juice
150 ml / 5 fl. oz tomato juice
a pinch of sea salt
a pinch of black pepper

TO SERVE
1 lime wedge
1 bacon rasher, fried until crispy

1. Put the 4 ice cubes into the cocktail shaker.
2. Pour the Worcestershire and hot sauce over the ice, then add the vodka, lemon juice and tomato juice.
3. Shake the cocktail shaker for at least 30 seconds.
4. Pour into a glass and add a pinch of salt and pepper.
5. Serve garnished with a small lime wedge and a rasher of fried bacon for decoration.

MAKES: **1 LITRE** | PREPARATION TIME: **5 MINS**

Mellow Lemon

ice cubes
250 ml / 9 fl. oz / 1 cup vodka
150 ml / 5 ½ fl. oz / ⅔ cup limoncello
250 ml / 9 fl. oz / 1 cup fresh lemon juice
4 shots sugar syrup
2 lemons, sliced
1 small bunch mint
chilled mineral water

1. Half-fill a large jug with ice cubes.
2. Add the vodka, limoncello, lemon juice, sugar syrup, sliced lemons and the bunch of mint.
3. Stir for 1 minute.
4. Top up the jug with mineral water to taste.
5. Pour into individual glasses and serve immediately.

Rosemary Vodka

5 sprigs of rosemary
4 shots vodka
2 shots lemon juice
2 shots lime juice
1 shot sugar syrup
8 ice cubes
10 slices cucumber
2 slices lemon, halved
chilled mineral water

1. Muddle three of the rosemary sprigs in the base of a cocktail shaker.
2. Add the vodka, lemon juice, lime juice, sugar syrup and ice. Shake vigorously for 1 minute.
3. Strain the cocktail into two small glass bottles and add the cucumber, sliced lemon and remaining rosemary.
4. Top up with mineral water to taste.

Fruity Cocktail

3 handfuls ice cubes
1 orange, cut into small chunks
2 apples, cut into small chunks
2 lemons, cut into wedges
2 limes, cut into wedges
1 handful mint leaves
5 shots Pimm's No.1
lemonade

1. Put ice into the jug and add the chopped fruit, mint leaves and Pimm's No.1.
2. Top up with lemonade.
3. Gently stir the mixture using a cocktail stirrer, ensuring it is thoroughly mixed together.
4. Pour into individual glasses with more ice.
5. Serve immediately.

SERVES: **2** | PREPARATION TIME: **5 MINS**

Cranberry Collins

1 handful fresh cranberries, plus extra to garnish
2 sprigs fresh rosemary, plus extra to garnish
4 shots London dry gin
2 shots fresh lemon juice
3 shots sugar syrup
8 ice cubes
crushed ice, to serve
soda water

1. Muddle the cranberries and rosemary in the base of a cocktail shaker to release the juice.
2. Add the gin, lemon juice, sugar syrup and ice cubes. Shake vigorously for 1 minute.
3. Fill two Collins glasses with crushed ice and strain the cocktail over the top.
4. Top up with soda water and garnish with rosemary sprigs and fresh cranberries.

Perky Cactus

3 ice cubes
1 shot tequila
½ shot blue curaçao
1 shot orange juice, strained
1 shot pineapple juice
1 shot lemon juice
½ shot peach juice

TO SERVE
extra ice cubes
1 peach wedge

1. Put the ice into the cocktail shaker.
2. Pour the tequila, blue curaçao, orange juice, pineapple juice, lemon juice and peach juice over the ice in the cocktail shaker, then shake for 30 seconds.
3. Strain into a glass and top with extra ice and a wedge of peach.

Frozen Kiwi Daiquiri

3 kiwi fruit, peeled and sliced
1 banana, peeled and sliced
3 shots white rum
1 shot kiwi liqueur
1 shot fresh lime juice
6 ice cubes
2 cherries

1. Reserve four slices of kiwi for the garnish. Spread the rest out on a baking tray with the banana and freeze for at least 2 hours. They can then be stored in a freezer bag for later use or used straight away.

2. Put the frozen fruit in a liquidizer with the rum, kiwi liqueur, lime juice and ice. Blend until very smooth.

3. Pour the cocktail into two glasses and garnish with kiwi slices and cherries threaded onto a skewer.

Mint Shake

1 ½ shots dark crème de cacao

1 shot white crème de menthe

1 shot Irish cream liqueur

1 tbsp unsweetened cocoa powder

1 scoop dark chocolate ice cream

1 scoop mint chocolate ice cream

4 ice cubes

TO SERVE

whipped cream

1 tbsp mint chocolate sauce

1. Measure the crème de cacao, crème de menthe and Irish cream liqueur into a liquidizer.
2. Add the cocoa, ice cream and ice cubes and blend for 30 seconds or until completely smooth.
3. Pour the cocktail into a glass and garnish with plenty of whipped cream and pour over some mint chocolate sauce.

SERVES: **1** | PREPARATION TIME: **5 MINS**

Greena Colada

2 handfuls spinach leaves, washed
1 handful kiwi chunks
3 ice cubes
2 shots white rum
2 shots coconut cream
pineapple juice

TO SERVE
sprig of mint

1. Put the spinach leaves and kiwi chunks in a blender and whizz for 30 seconds.
2. Put the ice cubes into the cocktail shaker.
3. Strain the blended fruit into the cocktail shaker then add the white rum and coconut cream over the ice in the shaker and shake for at least 30 seconds.
4. Pour into a glass and top up with pineapple juice. Stir well with a cocktail mixer.
5. Serve garnished with a sprig of mint.

Blackberry Vodka

6 ice cubes
4 blackberries, washed
2 shots vodka
3 shots lemonade
1 shot blackberry cordial
sprig of mint

1. Put the ice cubes and blackberries into the glass and pour in the vodka and lemonade.
2. Pour the cordial down one side of the glass, allowing it to float to the bottom.
3. Serve garnished with a sprig of mint.

Summer-Garita

3 ice cubes
1 shot lime juice
1 shot elderflower cordial
2 shots pineapple juice
pink lemonade

TO SERVE
2 strawberries, quartered
2 ice cubes

1. Put the ice cubes into the cocktail shaker.
2. Pour the lime juice, elderflower cordial and pineapple juice over the ice cubes in the cocktail shaker, then shake for 10 seconds.
3. Strain the mixture into a margarita glass, topping it up with pink lemonade.
4. Serve with some strawberry quarters and extra ice cubes.

SERVES: **1** | PREPARATION TIME: **5 MINS**

Vodka Martini

4 ice cubes
1 shot dry vermouth
2 shots vodka
2 olives

1. Put the ice cubes into the cocktail shaker.
2. Pour the dry vermouth and vodka into the cocktail shaker over the ice and shake for 20 seconds.
3. Pour the mixture into a martini glass, leaving the ice in the cocktail shaker.
4. Thread 2 olives onto a cocktail stick and balance it on the side of the glass.
5. Serve immediately with extra olives, if desired.

Citron Zorbet

2 handfuls ice cubes
1 shot lemon liqueur
1 shot vodka
1 shot lemon juice
1 tsp sugar syrup

1. Put the ice cubes into the cocktail shaker.
2. Add the lemon liqueur, vodka, lemon juice and sugar syrup, then shake for 20 seconds.
3. Strain into a glass and serve immediately.

SERVES: **1** | PREPARATION TIME: **5 MINS** | FREEZING TIME: **2 HOURS**

Frozen Mulberry Daiquiri

2 tbsp fresh mulberries
2 strawberries, quartered
½ banana, peeled and sliced
2 shots white rum
½ shot fresh lime juice
4 ice cubes
1 mint sprig, to garnish

1. Spread out the mulberries, strawberries and banana on a baking tray and freeze for at least 2 hours. They can then be stored in a freezer bag for later use or used straight away.
2. Put the frozen fruit in a liquidizer with the rum, lime juice and ice. Blend until very smooth.
3. Pour the cocktail into a glass and serve garnished with mint.

Clumsy Gardener

5 ice cubes
sprig of mint
2 shots gin
2 shots pineapple juice
1 shot lemon juice
½ shot of grenadine

TO SERVE
1 large pineapple wedge

1. Put the ice cubes into the cocktail shaker.
2. Add the mint, gin, pineapple juice, lemon juice and grenadine to the cocktail shaker, then shake for 30 seconds.
3. Pour into a glass or jar.
4. Serve garnished with a large wedge of pineapple.

SERVES: 1 | PREPARATION TIME: 5 MINS

Purple Rain

2 handfuls blueberries
4 handfuls crushed ice
½ shot vodka
½ shot light rum
½ shot gin
½ shot bourbon whisky
½ shot blue curaçao
lemonade

1. Put the blueberries and 2 handfuls of crushed ice in a blender and whizz for 20 seconds.
2. Put the remaining 2 handfuls of crushed ice into the cocktail shaker.
3. Pour the vodka, light rum, gin, bourbon whisky and blue curaçao over the crushed ice in the cocktail shaker, then shake for 20 seconds.
4. Pour into a glass and add the blended blueberries.
5. Stir well and serve immediately.

SERVES: **1** | PREPARATION TIME: **5 MINS**

Cosmopolitan

2 ice cubes
1 shot vodka
1 shot lime juice
1 shot triple sec
3 shots cranberry juice

TO SERVE
1 watermelon wedge or lime wedge
sprig of mint

1. Put the ice into the cocktail shaker.
2. Add the vodka, lime juice, triple sec and cranberry juice over the ice, then shake for 20 seconds.
3. Pour into a martini glass.
4. Serve immediately, garnished with a watermelon wedge or lime wedge and a sprig of mint.

P.S. I Love You

3 ice cubes
½ shot dark rum
½ shot amaretto
1 shot Irish cream liqueur
½ shot coffee liqueur
2 shots cream
3 shots milk

1. Put the ice cubes into the cocktail shaker.
2. Pour the dark rum, amaretto, Irish cream liqueur, coffee liqueur, cream and milk over the ice in the cocktail shaker, then shake for 20 seconds.
3. Strain into a glass and serve immediately.

Passion Fruit Punch

2 shots passion fruit juice
3 shots white rum
1 shot sugar syrup
1 shot lime juice
6 ice cubes
Prosecco, to top up
1 passion fruit, halved
a few sprigs mint

1. Put the passion fruit juice in a cocktail shaker with the rum, sugar syrup, lime juice and ice. Shake vigorously for 1 minute.
2. Strain the cocktail into a tall glass and top up with Prosecco.
3. Scoop the passion fruit seeds into the glass and garnish with plenty of mint.

SERVES: **1** | PREPARATION TIME: **5 MINS**

Gin and Tonic

150 ml / 5 fl. oz tonic water, chilled
2 shots gin

TO SERVE
1 handful cucumber slices
½ lemon, thinly sliced
½ lime, thinly sliced

1. Pour the chilled tonic water and gin into a glass.
2. Stir well.
3. Serve with several cucumber, lemon and lime slices.
4. For added flavour, add a sprig of rosemary or thyme if desired.

Fruity Manhattan

5 ice cubes

1 shot bourbon whisky

1 shot sweet red vermouth

1 handful strawberries, chopped into large chunks

1 dash Angostura bitters

1. Put the ice into the cocktail shaker.
2. Add the bourbon whisky, sweet red vermouth and Angostura bitters.
3. Strain into a glass and add the strawberries.
4. Serve immediately, garnished with mint sprigs if desired.

SERVES: **1** | PREPARATION TIME: **5 MINS**

Mai Tai

2 handfuls ice cubes
½ shot almond syrup
½ shot sugar syrup
½ shot dark rum
1 shot light rum
2 shots orange curaçao
fresh lime juice

TO SERVE
1 cherry
1 pineapple wedge
2 spikes cut from the pineapple crown

1. Put the ice into the cocktail shaker.
2. Pour the almond syrup, sugar syrup, dark rum, light rum and 1 shot of the orange curaçao over the ice in the shaker, then shake for 20 seconds.
3. Pour into a glass and top up with lime juice and pour over the second shot of orange curaçao.
4. Serve immediately, garnished with a cherry, wedge of pineapple and a couple of the spikes from the pineapple crown.

Margarita

3 ice cubes
2 shots fresh lime juice
2 shots tequila
1 shot triple sec
a pinch of salt

TO SERVE
salt, for the rim of the glass
1 lime slice

1. Put the ice into the cocktail shaker.
2. Pour the lime juice, tequila and triple sec over the ice in the shaker, then shake for 10 seconds.
3. Dip the rim of the margarita glass in water, then salt.
4. Pour the mixture into the glass, leaving the ice in the cocktail shaker.
5. Serve garnished with a lime slice.

Rainbow Punch

4 ice cubes
2 shots grapefruit juice
3 shots cranberry juice
2 shots orange juice
1 shot lemon juice
1 shot vodka
a dash grenadine
1 handful redcurrants or cranberries
1 lemon slice

1. Put 2 ice cubes into the cocktail shaker.
2. Pour the grapefruit juice, cranberry juice, orange juice, lemon juice, vodka and grenadine over the ice cubes in the cocktail shaker, then shake for 20 seconds.
3. Strain into a glass and add the remaining 2 ice cubes, the redcurrants and a slice of lemon.

SERVES: **1** | PREPARATION TIME: **5-8 MINS**

Ultimate Rum Hot Chocolate

2 shots coconut rum
hot chocolate, made with milk

TO SERVE
whipped cream
2 tsp chocolate shavings (optional)
2 walnuts (optional)
deluxe chocolates (optional)

1. Pour the coconut rum into a thick, heat-proof glass.
2. Add the hot chocolate and stir well, ensuring the hot chocolate is fully warmed.
3. Top with whipped cream and chocolate shavings, walnuts and chocolates, if desired.
4. Serve immediately.

Irish Coffee

2 tsp brown sugar

1 tsp coffee granules

150 ml / 5 fl. oz near-boiling water

2 shots Irish cream liqueur

whipped cream

TO SERVE

1 tsp cocoa powder

1. Stir the sugar and coffee granules together in a thick, heatproof glass with 150 ml of near-boiling water.
2. Stir well to ensure it is mixed.
3. Add the Irish cream liqueur and stir again.
4. Float the whipped cream on the top and serve immediately, sprinkled with cocoa powder if desired.

Sex on the Beach

1 handful ice cubes
2 shots vodka
1 shot peach schnapps
3 shots orange juice
3 shots cranberry juice

TO SERVE
2 raspberries
sprig of mint

1. Put ice into the shaker.
2. Add the vodka and peach schnapps over the ice in the shaker, then shake for 10 seconds.
3. Pour into a glass and top up with orange and cranberry juice.
4. Serve immediately with the raspberries and a sprig of mint.

Berry Nice

4 ice cubes
1 shot of cherry liqueur
1 shot of cranberry juice
a pinch of salt
Champagne

TO SERVE
1 handful redcurrants
1 lime slice

1. Put the ice cubes into the cocktail shaker.
2. Pour the cherry liqueur and cranberry juice over the ice cubes in the cocktail shaker, then shake for 10 seconds.
3. Dip the rim of the glass in water, then salt. The salt can be substituted for sugar if a sweeter alternative is desired.
4. Strain the cocktail mixture into a glass and top up with Champagne.
5. Serve garnished with a lime slice and redcurrants.

Watermelon Rum

3 handfuls watermelon chunks, deseeded
1 tsp sugar
1 shot lime juice
1 shot lemon juice
1 shot white rum
soda water

TO SERVE
1 handful mint leaves
1 slice lemon

1. Put the watermelon chunks in a juicer according to the manufacturer's instructions.
2. Mix the sugar, lemon juice and lime juice together in a glass.
3. Add the rum, watermelon juice and ice.
4. Top up with soda water.
5. Serve with mint leaves and a slice of lemon.

SERVES: **1** | PREPARATION TIME: **5 MINS**

Pink Flamingo

2 handfuls crushed ice
2 shots white rum
1 shot grenadine
1 shot lime juice
2 shots pineapple juice

TO SERVE
sprig of mint

1. Put the crushed ice into the cocktail shaker.
2. Pour the white rum, grenadine, lime juice and pineapple juice over the crushed ice in the cocktail shaker, then shake for 10 seconds.
3. Pour into a tall glass and serve immediately, garnished with mint or a lime slice.

SERVES: **1** | PREPARATION TIME: **5 MINS**

Woo Woo

5 ice cubes
1 shot peach schnapps
2 shots vodka
5 shots cranberry juice

TO SERVE
1 lime slice

1. Put the 5 ice cubes into the cocktail shaker.
2. Pour the peach schnapps and vodka over the ice in the shaker, then shake for at least 20 seconds.
3. Pour into a tall glass and top up with the cranberry juice.
4. Serve with a slice of lime.

SERVES: **1** | PREPARATION TIME: **5 MINS**

White Russian

1 large ice cube
2 shots vodka
1 shot coffee liqueur
4 shots cream

1. Put the ice cube into the cocktail shaker.
2. Add the vodka and coffee liqueur over the ice in the shaker, then shake for 10 seconds.
3. Pour into a glass and gently pour in the cream.
4. Allow the ice to cool the cocktail for 2-3 minutes before drinking.

Vodka Zing

5 ice cubes
1 shot vodka
½ shot lime juice
½ shot lemon juice
cloudy lemonade

TO SERVE
1 lime slice
sprig of mint

1. Put the ice cubes into the cocktail shaker.
2. Pour the vodka, lime juice and lemon juice into the cocktail shaker over the ice and shake for 10 seconds.
3. Pour the mixture into a glass and top up with cloudy lemonade.
4. Serve garnished with a lime slice and a sprig of mint.

Berry Shake

1 handful crushed ice
1 handful frozen raspberries
1 handful frozen strawberries
1 handful blueberries
4 shots semi-skimmed milk
2 shots orange juice, chilled
1 shot vodka
1 shot lime juice

TO SERVE
2 frozen raspberries
2 blueberries

1. Put all the ingredients in a blender and whizz for at least 30 seconds or until completely blended and smooth.
2. Pour the blended mixture into a glass.
3. Serve garnished with a couple of raspberries and blueberries.

SERVES: **1** | PREPARATION TIME: **5 MINS**

Pink Martini

2 shots London dry gin
½ shot sweet white vermouth
2 shots pink grapefruit juice
1 shot cranberry juice
6 ice cubes

TO SERVE
1 curl lime zest

1. Put the gin, vermouth, grapefruit juice and cranberry juice in a mixing glass with the ice cubes.
2. Stir briskly for 30 seconds, then strain the cocktail into a martini glass.
3. Garnish with a curl of lime zest and serve immediately.

SERVES: 1 | PREPARATION TIME: 5 MINS

Pineapple Margarita

2 handfuls ice cubes

2 shots tequila

1 shot triple sec

3 shots pineapple juice

½ shot lime juice

1 tsp salt

lime wedge

1. Put the ice cubes into the cocktail shaker.
2. Pour the tequila, triple sec, pineapple juice and lime juice over the ice cubes in the cocktail shaker, then shake for 20 seconds.
3. Rub the lime wedge around the rim of the glass, then dip in salt.
4. Pour the cocktail mixture into the martini glass and add more ice cubes, if desired.

Purple Lagoon

4 ice cubes
2 shots vodka
2 shots blackberry cordial
lemonade
1 handfuls blackberries

TO SERVE
1 lemon slice
sprig of mint

1. Put the ice cubes into the cocktail shaker.
2. Pour the vodka and blackberry cordial over the ice in the shaker, then shake for 10 seconds.
3. Pour into a glass and top up with lemonade.
4. Add the handful of blackberries and lemon slice.
5. Serve immediately, garnished with a sprig of mint.

Pick Me Up

1 shot brandy
1 shot orange juice, chilled
1 shot peach juice, chilled
Champagne
1 handful ice cubes

1. Pour the brandy, orange juice and peach juice into a flute glass.
2. Gently add the ice cubes.
3. Top up with Champagne, being careful that it does not overflow.
4. Stir thoroughly then serve immediately.

MAKES: **750 ML** | PREPARATION TIME: **5 MINS**

Strawberry and Blood Orange Punch

10 ripe strawberries
250 ml / 9 fl. oz / 1 cup blood orange
 juice, chilled
175 ml / 6 fl. oz / ⅔ cup London dry gin
100 ml / 3 ½ fl. oz / ½ cup red vermouth
2 limes, juiced
100 ml / 3 ½ fl. oz / ½ cup sugar syrup
2 egg whites
ice cubes, to serve

1. Put all of the ingredients, except the
   ice, in a liquidizer and blend until
   smooth and frothy.
2. Pour the punch into an ice-filled jug
   and stir well to chill.
3. Serve immediately.

Extra Pineapple Piña Colada

1 handful pineapple chunks
4 ice cubes
1 shot white rum
5 shots pineapple juice
2 shots coconut cream

TO SERVE
1 pineapple wedge

1. Put the pineapple chunks in a blender and whizz for 20 seconds. Pour into a glass to fill the bottom half.
2. Put the ice cubes into the cocktail shaker.
3. Pour the white rum, pineapple juice and coconut cream over the ice in the shaker and shake for at least 30 seconds.
4. Pour gently into a glass to fill it to the top, leaving the blended pineapple chunks to sit in the bottom of the glass.
5. Serve garnished with a pineapple wedge.

SERVES: **1** | PREPARATION TIME: **5 MINS**

All American Fizz

2 handfuls strawberries
5 ice cubes
1 shot gin
1 shot brandy
1 shot lemon juice
½ shot grenadine
soda water

TO SERVE
2 handfuls crushed ice

1. Process the strawberries through a juicer according to the manufacturer's instructions.
2. Put the ice cubes into the cocktail shaker and pour over the strained strawberry juice, gin, brandy, lemon juice and grenadine.
3. Pour into a glass and top up with soda water.
4. Serve immediately with crushed ice.

Pomegranate Punch

4 ice cubes

1 tsp sugar syrup

1 shot lime juice

6 shots pomegranate juice

1 tbsp pomegranate seeds

lemonade

TO SERVE

1 tbsp pomegranate seeds

sprig of mint

1. Put the ice cubes into the cocktail shaker.
2. Pour the sugar syrup, lime juice, pomegranate juice and 1 tablespoon of pomegranate seeds over the ice cubes in the cocktail shaker, then shake for 20 seconds.
3. Pour into a glass and top up with lemonade.
4. Serve garnished with more pomegranate seeds and a sprig of mint.

Peachsecco

2 shots white rum
3 shots peach iced tea, chilled
prosecco

TO SERVE
1 handful raspberries, preferably frozen
1 handful peach wedges

1. Pour the white rum and peach iced tea into the cocktail shaker, then shake for 10 seconds.
2. Pour into a glass and top up with prosecco.
3. Serve immediately, floating the raspberries and peach wedges in the cocktail.

Singapore Sling

5 ice cubes
2 shots of pineapple juice
½ shot of Benedictine
½ shot of grenadine
½ shot of Cointreau
1 shot of gin
1 shot of cherry brandy
soda water

TO SERVE
1 handful redcurrants (optional)

1. Put the ice cubes into the cocktail shaker.
2. Add the pineapple juice, Benedictine, grenadine, Cointreau, gin and cherry brandy over the ice in the shaker, then shake for 20 seconds.
3. Pour into a tall glass and top up with soda water.
4. Serve sprinkled with redcurrants, if desired.

Starlust

2 ice cubes
3 shots pineapple juice
1 shot vodka
1 tsp sugar syrup
2 pineapple wedges, peeled
1 star fruit, finely sliced and de-seeded
soda water

TO SERVE
sprig of mint

1. Put the ice cubes into the cocktail shaker.
2. Put the pineapple juice, vodka, sugar syrup, pineapple wedges and star fruit in the cocktail shaker, then shake well for 20 seconds, allowing the flavour to come out of the fruit.
3. Pour the cocktail into a glass and top up with soda water.
4. Serve garnished with a sprig of mint.

Harvey Wallbanger

3 ice cubes
1 shot vodka
½ shot lemon juice
fresh orange juice, strained
1 shot Galliano

1. Put the ice cubes into a glass.
2. Add the vodka and lemon juice then top up with orange juice.
3. Pour the Galliano into the mixture.
4. Serve immediately.

Mojitwhoa

10 mint leaves or 5 mint sprigs
1 tsp sugar
2 shots white rum
2 shots lime juice
1 lime, cut into small chunks
3 shots apple juice, chilled
½ apple, cut into thin slices
5 ice cubes
soda water

1. Mash the mint and sugar together in a glass or jar.
2. Add the rum, lime juice, lime chunks, apple juice, apple slices and ice.
3. Top up with soda water, stir well and serve immediately.

Raspberry and Mint Julep

2 sprigs mint
2 shots raspberry eau de vie
1 shot sugar syrup
8 ice cubes
1 handful fresh raspberries
chilled mineral water

1. Put the mint, eau de vie, sugar syrup and ice in a cocktail shaker and shake vigorously for 1 minute.
2. Put the raspberries in a rocks glass and pour in the cocktail without straining.
3. Top up with chilled mineral water to taste.

SERVES: **1** | PREPARATION TIME: **5 MINS**

Long Island Iced Tea

½ shot vodka
½ shot tequila
½ shot white rum
½ shot gin
½ shot triple sec
½ shot lime juice
½ shot lemon juice
7 ice cubes
1 lemon wedge
1 sprig rosemary
cola

1. Put the vodka, tequila, rum, gin, triple sec, lime juice and lemon juice in a cocktail shaker with six of the ice cubes.
2. Shake vigorously for 1 minute, then strain into a rocks glass.
3. Add the lemon wedge rosemary and remaining ice cube, then top up with cola.

SERVES: **6** | PREPARATION TIME: **5 MINS**

Sangria

10 ice cubes
1 bottle red wine
1 orange, cut into wedges
1 lemon, cut into wedges
2 tbsp sugar
3 shots brandy
300 ml / 10 fl. oz soda water

TO SERVE
1 lime slice
additional fruit to taste (optional)

1. Put the ice cubes into a large jug and pour in the red wine.
2. Squeeze the juice from the orange and lemon wedges into the jug then add the wedges themselves.
3. Add the sugar, brandy and soda water.
4. Stir well and pour into individual glasses.
5. Serve immediately.

SERVES: **2** | PREPARATION TIME: **10 MINS** | FREEZING TIME: **2 HOURS**

Layered Raspberry and Mango Daiquiri

150 g / 5 ½ oz / 1 cup fresh raspberries
½ mango, peeled and diced
1 banana, peeled and sliced
1 passion fruit, halved
4 shots white rum
8 ice cubes
1 shot fresh lime juice
2 slices kiwi

1. Reserve two raspberries for the garnish. Spread the rest out on a baking tray with the mango and banana and freeze for at least 2 hours. They can then be stored in a freezer bag for later use or used straight away.

2. Put the frozen raspberries in a liquidizer and add half the banana, half the rum and half the ice.

3. Whizz in the liquidizer until smooth, then divide between two glasses.

4. Give the liquidizer a quick rinse out, then scoop in the passion fruit seeds and add the lime juice, frozen mango and the rest of the banana, rum and ice.

5. Blend until smooth, then gently layer on top of the raspberry daiquiri. Try not to stir the mixture together as this will muddle the colours.

6. Garnish with raspberries and kiwi slices, then serve immediately.

SERVES: **1** | PREPARATION TIME: **5 MINS**

Raspberry Limoncello Fizz

1 shot vodka

2 shots limoncello

1 shot fresh lemon juice

6 ice cubes

Prosecco, to top up

6 fresh raspberries

1 sprig mint

1. Measure the vodka, limoncello and lemon juice into a cocktail shaker and add the ice.
2. Shake vigorously for 1 minute, then strain into a highball glass.
3. Top up with Prosecco and float the raspberries and mint on top.

SERVES: **2** | PREPARATION TIME: **5 MINS**

Cosmopoligin

2 shots London dry gin
2 shots triple sec
3 shots cranberry juice
1 shot fresh lime juice
6 ice cubes

1. Put all of the ingredients in a cocktail shaker and shake vigorously for 1 minute.
2. Strain into two martini glasses and serve immediately.

Alabama Slammer

4 ice cubes
½ shot bourbon whisky
½ shot amaretto
½ shot sloe gin
2 shots orange juice

TO SERVE
1 orange wedge

1. Put the ice into the cocktail shaker.
2. Pour the bourbon whisky, amaretto, sloe gin and orange juice over the ice in the cocktail shaker, then shake for 10 seconds.
3. Strain into a glass and serve immediately, garnished with an orange wedge.

Blue Hawaiian

5 ice cubes
6 shots light rum
2 shots coconut milk
3 shots blue curaçao
pineapple juice

TO SERVE
3 lemon slices
2 handfuls ice cubes

1. Put 5 ice cubes into the cocktail shaker.
2. Pour the light rum, coconut milk and 2 shots of the blue curaçao and the pineapple juice over the ice in the cocktail shaker, then shake for 30 seconds.
3. Pour the mixture into a large jug.
4. Top up with coconut milk.
5. Pour the final shot of blue curaçao down the inside of the jug so that it sits at the bottom and gives a gradient effect.
6. Top up with jug with more ice cubes and some lemon slices.
7. Serve immediately.

SERVES: **1** | PREPARATION TIME: **5 MINS**

Summer Field

2 kiwis, peeled
1 shot gin
1 shot advocaat
2 shots orange juice
2 shots passion fruit juice (or tropical juice)

1. Put the kiwis in a blender and whizz for at least 30 seconds or until completely blended and smooth.
2. Meanwhile, pour the gin, advocaat, orange juice and passion fruit juice into a glass or jar.
3. Add the blended kiwi to the cocktail mixture then stir thoroughly.
4. Serve immediately with crushed ice, if desired.

Green Heaven

4 sprigs mint

4 shots sake

2 shots vodka

2 shots triple sec

2 shots fresh lime juice

1 shot sugar syrup

100 ml / 3 ½ fl. oz / ½ cup chilled mineral water

2 tsp matcha green tea powder

2 handfuls ice cubes

½ lime, sliced

1. Muddle half of the mint in the base of a cocktail shaker. Add the sake, vodka, triple sec, lime juice, sugar syrup, water and matcha.
2. Add a handful of ice cubes and shake vigorously for 1 minute.
3. Divide the rest of the ice between two glasses and add the sliced lime and remaining mint sprigs. Strain over the cocktail and serve immediately.

Piña Berry Colada

1 handful blueberries, washed

1 handful blackberries, washed

1 handful crushed ice

1 shot white rum

2 shots coconut cream

pineapple juice

TO SERVE

sprig of mint

1. Put the blueberries and blackberries in a blender and whizz for 30 seconds.
2. Put the crushed ice into the cocktail shaker.
3. Pour the blended berries, white rum and coconut cream over the crushed ice in the shaker and shake for at least 30 seconds.
4. Pour into a glass and top up with pineapple juice.
5. Serve garnished with a sprig of mint.

SERVES: **2** | PREPARATION TIME: **5 MINS**

Mojito Royale

6 fresh mint leaves, torn, plus extra
  sprigs to garnish
1 lime, sliced
4 shots white rum
1 ½ shots fresh lime juice
1 shot sugar syrup
crushed ice
Champagne, to top up

1. Put the mint in a cocktail shaker with
   half of the sliced lime.
2. Add the rum, lime juice, sugar syrup
   and a scoop of crushed ice and shake
   vigorously for 30 seconds.
3. Divide between two Collins glasses
   and add more crushed ice to fill.
4. Top up with Champagne and garnish
   with extra mint sprigs and the rest of
   the sliced lime.

berry Mojito

rigs spearmint, plus extra to garnish
lime, cut into wedges
6 strawberries, quartered
4 shots white rum
2 shots fresh lime juice
ice cubes
pineapple juice
soda water

1. Put the mint, lime wedges and strawberries in two high-ball glasses and muddle to release the juice.
2. Add the rum and lime and stir well, then fill the glass with ice cubes.
3. Top up with soda and stir, then serve garnished with the extra mint.

SERVES: **1** | PREPARATION TIME: **5 MINS**

Lychee Martini

2 shots vodka
2 shots lychee juice
2 shots pink grapefruit juice, chilled
8 ice cubes

TO SERVE
½ fresh lychee

1. Put the vodka, lychee juice and grapefruit juice in a cocktail shaker.
2. Add the ice to the shaker and shake vigorously for 1 minute.
3. Strain into a coupe glass and serve immediately, garnished with half a lychee.

Marma-rita

1 tsp salt
1 tsp caster (superfine) sugar
1 lemon wedge
2 shots tequila reposado
1 shot triple sec
1 shot fresh orange juice
1 shot fresh lemon juice
6 ice cubes

1. Mix the salt and sugar on a saucer. Moisten the rim of a coupe glass with the lemon wedge, then dip it in the salt and sugar mix to coat.
2. Put the rest of the ingredients in a cocktail shaker and shake vigorously for 1 minute.
3. Strain into the glass and serve immediately.

Casablanca

6 ice cubes
2 shots of white rum
½ shot of cherry liqueur
1 shot of triple sec
1 shot of lemon juice
1 orange, cut into wedges

TO SERVE
1 lemon wedge

1. Put the ice into the cocktail shaker.
2. Pour the white rum, cherry liqueur, triple sec and lemon juice over the ice in the cocktail shaker, then shake for 20 seconds.
3. Pour into a glass and squeeze the juice from the orange wedges into the cocktail.
4. Serve immediately, garnished with a lemon wedge.

SERVES: **1** | PREPARATION TIME: **5 MINS**

Bramble Julep

2 sprigs mint
1 slice lemon, halved
1 shot raspberry eau de vie
1 shot blackberry eau de vie
1 shot sugar syrup
8 ice cubes
1 handful fresh raspberries
3 blackberries
chilled mineral water

1. Put the mint, lemon, eau de vies, sugar syrup and ice in a cocktail shaker and shake vigorously for 1 minute.
2. Put the raspberries in a rocks glass and pour in the cocktail without straining.
3. Top up with chilled mineral water.
4. Garnish with the blackberries and serve immediately.

Fruity Gin Fizz

2 shots London dry gin
1 shot fresh lemon juice
½ shot sugar syrup
12 ice cubes
1 strawberry, sliced
2 slices orange, halved
½ tsp fresh thyme leaves
soda water

1. Put the gin, lemon juice and sugar syrup in a cocktail shaker with half of the ice cubes. Shake vigorously for 1 minute.
2. Put the strawberry, orange and thyme in a mason jar glass, then add the rest of the ice.
3. Strain the cocktail into the glass and top up with soda water.

Frozen Tropical Daiquiri

½ ripe mango, peeled and cubed
1 banana, peeled and sliced
4 shots white rum
1 shot orange liqueur
1 orange, juiced
1 shot fresh lime juice
8 ice cubes
1 passion fruit, halved

1. Spread out the mango on a baking tray with the banana and freeze for at least 2 hours. They can then be stored in a freezer bag for later use or used straight away.
2. Put the frozen fruit in a liquidizer with the rum, orange juice, lime juice and ice. Blend until very smooth.
3. Pour the cocktail into two glasses and scoop the passion fruit seeds on top.

SERVES: 1 | PREPARATION TIME: 5 MINS

Vodka Sour

2 shots vodka

1 shot fresh lemon juice

¾ shot sugar syrup

8 ice cubes

1 slice lemon

1. Put the vodka, lemon juice and sugar syrup in a cocktail shaker with six of the ice cubes.
2. Shake vigorously for 1 minute.
3. Wrap the lemon slice around the other two ice cubes and place in an old-fashioned glass.
4. Strain the cocktail into the glass and serve immediately.

SERVES: **1** | PREPARATION TIME: **10 MINS**

Rosemary and Elderflower Collins

1 lemon

2 sprigs fresh rosemary, plus extra
  to garnish

2 shots London dry gin

1 shot fresh lemon juice

1 ½ shots elderflower cordial

8 ice cubes

ice cubes, to serve

soda water

1. Use a vegetable peeler to shave a
long ribbon of lemon zest and
reserve, then cut the rest of the lemon
into cubes. Muddle the cubed lemon
with the rosemary in the base of a
cocktail shaker.

2. Add the gin, lemon juice, elderflower
cordial and ice cubes.

3. Shake vigorously for 1 minute.

4. Fill a Collins glass with ice cubes and
strain the cocktail over the top.

5. Top up with soda water, then wrap
the reserved ribbon of lemon zest
around a rosemary sprig and use
to garnish the drink.

Fuchsia Lemonade

ice cubes

3 shots raspberry liqueur

2 shots blue curaçao

150 ml / 5 ½ fl. oz / ⅔ cup fresh lemon juice

3 shots sugar syrup

1 lemon, sliced

75 g / 2 ½ oz / ½ cup strawberries, quartered

soda water

TO SERVE

mint sprigs

1. Half-fill a large jug with ice cubes. Add the rest of the ingredients, apart from the soda water, and stir for 1 minute.
2. Top up the jug with soda water, then pour into glasses.
3. Garnish with mint sprigs and serve immediately.

Cucumber and Mint Fizz

5 cm (2 in) cucumber, diced, plus 1 slice to garnish

6 mint leaves

2 shots London dry gin

8 ice cubes

tonic water

1. Muddle the cucumber and mint in the bottom of a cocktail shaker.
2. Add the gin and six ice cubes and shake vigorously for 1 minute.
3. Strain into a glass and add the remaining two ice cubes.
4. Top up with tonic water to taste.
5. Garnish with a cucumber slice and serve.

SERVES: **1** | PREPARATION TIME: **5 MINS**

Blue Lagoon

2 ice cubes
2 shots vodka
1 shot blue curaçao
lemonade

TO SERVE
1 lemon slice

1. Put the ice cubes into the cocktail shaker.
2. Pour the vodka and blue curaçao over the ice in the shaker, then shake for 10 seconds.
3. Leaving the ice cubes in the shaker, pour the mixture into a glass and top up with lemonade.
4. Serve immediately, garnished with a slice of lemon.

SERVES: **1** | PREPARATION TIME: **5 MINS**

Pimm's Cup

2 shots Pimm's No.1 Cup
4 slices cucumber
3 orange wedges
6 ice cubes
lemonade

1. Measure the Pimm's into a highball glass.
2. Add the cucumber, orange and ice to the glass, then stir gently to mix.
3. Top up with lemonade.
4. Serve immediately.

Hot Apple Toddy

250 ml / 9 fl. oz / 1 cup apple juice
2 cinnamon sticks, halved
2 star anise
4 cloves
6 brown sugar cubes
4 shots whisky
½ eating apple, sliced

1. Put the apple juice in a small saucepan with the cinnamon, star anise, cloves and sugar cubes.
2. Stir over a low heat to dissolve the sugar, then bring to a simmer.
3. Measure the whisky into two glass mugs and add the sliced apple.
4. Divide the mulled apple juice and spices between the cups.
5. Serve immediately.

MAKES: **1 LITRE** | PREPARATION TIME: **10 MINS**

Cucumber, Lime and Thyme Cooler

1 cucumber
ice cubes
1 lime, sliced
1 small bunch fresh thyme
250 ml / 9 fl. oz / 1 cup vodka
250 ml / 9 fl. oz / 1 cup fresh lime juice
100 ml / 3 ½ fl. oz / ½ cup sugar syrup
mineral water

1. Peel two thirds of the cucumber, then process it through a juicer.
2. Use the vegetable peeler to slice the rest of the cucumber into very thin ribbons.
3. Half-fill a large jug with ice cubes and add the cucumber ribbons, lime and thyme.
4. Add the rest of the cucumber juice and the rest of the ingredients and stir for 1 minute.
5. Top up the jug with mineral water and serve immediately.

Pineapple Mojito

4 fresh mint leaves, torn
1 lime, cut into wedges
2 shots golden rum
1 shot fresh lime juice
crushed ice
pineapple juice

TO SERVE
1 wedge fresh pineapple
sprig of mint

1. Put the torn mint and lime wedges in a high-ball glass and muddle to release the juice.
2. Add the rum and lime and stir well, then fill the glass with crushed ice.
3. Top up with pineapple juice and stir.
4. Serve garnished with the wedge of pineapple and mint.

SERVES: **2** | PREPARATION TIME: **5 MINS**

Tom Collins

4 shots Old Tom gin
2 shots fresh lemon juice
1 shot sugar syrup
8 ice cubes
crushed ice
soda water

TO SERVE
2 lemon wedges

1. Put the gin in a cocktail shaker with the lemon juice, sugar syrup and ice cubes. Shake vigorously for 1 minute.
2. Fill two Collins glasses with crushed ice and strain the cocktail over the top.
3. Top up with soda water.
4. Garnish with lemon wedges and serve.

Mocktails

SERVES: **1** | PREPARATION TIME: **5 MINS**

Sunset Island

3 ice cubes

3 shots pineapple juice

5 shots grapefruit juice

2 tsp sugar syrup

lemonade

TO SERVE

3 spikes cut from the pineapple crown

3 cm (1 in) orange peel

3 ice cubes

1. Put the ice cubes into the cocktail shaker.
2. Pour the pineapple juice, grapefruit juice and sugar syrup over the ice in the cocktail shaker, then shake for 20 seconds.
3. Pour into a tall glass and top up with lemonade.
4. Serve garnished with some spikes cut from the pineapple crown, some orange peel and more ice cubes, if desired.

Tropical Mojito

1 tbsp mint syrup
1 handful pineapple chunks
1 tsp sugar
2 shots lime juice
3 shots pineapple juice
1 handful ice cubes
soda water

TO SERVE
sprig of mint
2 pineapple chunks

1. Mash the mint syrup, pineapple chunks and sugar together in a glass.
2. Add the lime juice, pineapple juice and ice cubes.
3. Top up with soda water.
4. Serve garnished with a sprig of mint and pineapple chunks on a wooden skewer.

Chocolate Pick Me Up

2 tbsp unsweetened cocoa powder
200 ml / 7 fl. oz / ¾ cup semi-skimmed milk
1 tbsp chocolate milkshake powder
2 shots espresso, cooled
8 ice cubes
1 square dark chocolate

1. Moisten the rim of two martini glasses with water and dip them in cocoa powder.
2. Put the excess cocoa powder in a cocktail shaker with the milk, milkshake powder, espresso and ice. Shake vigorously for 1 minute, then strain into the glass.
3. Grate the chocolate over the top and serve immediately.

Berry Heaven

10 frozen raspberries
5 frozen strawberries
5 ice cubes
1 shot pineapple juice, strained
1 shot orange juice, strained
4 shots cranberry juice
3 sprigs of mint

TO SERVE
extra ice cubes

1. Process the raspberries and strawberries through a juicer according to the manufacturer's instructions.
2. Meanwhile, put the ice cubes into the cocktail shaker.
3. Pour the pineapple juice, orange juice, cranberry juice and mint over the ice in the cocktail shaker, then shake for 20 seconds.
4. Strain the mixture from the shaker into a tall glass, leaving the sprigs of mint in the shaker.
5. Add more ice to the glass and serve immediately.

SERVES: **1** | PREPARATION TIME: **5 MINS**

What-a-Ma-Ma

1 tsp sugar syrup
1 tsp mint syrup
1 shot lime juice
1 shot lemon juice
cloudy lemonade, chilled
3 handfuls watermelon chunks
1 handful strawberry chunks

TO SERVE
sprig of mint

1. Pour the sugar syrup, mint syrup, lime juice and lemon juice into the cocktail shaker, then shake for 10 seconds.
2. Strain into a glass or jar and top up with the cloudy lemonade.
3. Add the watermelon and strawberry chunks to the cocktail, stirring well.
4. Serve garnished with a sprig of mint.

SERVES: **1** | PREPARATION TIME: **5 MINS**

Lime-O-Scene

3 handfuls mint leaves, crushed
1 tsp sugar syrup
2 shots lime juice
1 shot lime cordial
3 shots lemonade
1 handful ice cubes
1 lime, cut into wedges

TO SERVE
1 lime slice

1. Mash the mint leaves and sugar syrup together in a glass.
2. Add in the lime juice, lime cordial and lemonade. Stir well.
3. Add the ice cubes and lime wedges.
4. Serve immediately, garnished with a lime slice.

Summer Tart

5 ice cubes
2 shots lemon juice
150 ml / 5 fl. oz apple juice
½ lemon, cut into wedges

TO SERVE
6 apple slices

1. Put the ice into the cocktail shaker.
2. Add the lemon juice and apple juice over the ice in the shaker, then shake for 20 seconds.
3. Pour into a glass and squeeze the lemon wedges into the mixture to add extra fresh lemon juice.
4. Serve immediately, garnished with apple slices.

SERVES: **1** | PREPARATION TIME: **5 MINS**

Raspberry Mojito

2 handfuls raspberries

1 tbsp mint syrup

1 tsp sugar

2 shots lime juice

1 shot apple juice

1 handful ice cubes

soda water

TO SERVE

1 lime slice

1 handful mint leaves

1 raspberry

1. Put the raspberries in a blender and whizz for 30 seconds.
2. Meanwhile, mash the mint syrup and sugar together in a glass.
3. Add the lime juice, apple juice, blended raspberries and ice.
4. Top up with soda water.
5. Serve garnished with a lime slice, mint leaves and a raspberry.

SERVES: **2** | PREPARATION TIME: **5 MINS**

Virgin Berry Margarita

2 tbsp pink sugar crystals
75 g / 2 ½ oz / ½ cup frozen redcurrants, strawberries and raspberries
250 ml / 9 fl. oz / 1 cup semi-skimmed milk
1 tbsp runny honey

1. Moisten the rim of two martini glasses with water, then dip in the sugar crystals.
2. Put the frozen redcurrant, strawberries, raspberries, milk and honey in a liquidizer and blend until very smooth.
3. Divide between the glasses and serve immediately.

Apple Mocktail Mule

3 apples
1 cm ginger
2 shots lime juice
soda water
1 handful ice cubes
1 lime slice
sprig of mint

1. Process the apples and ginger through a juicer according to the manufacturer's instructions.
2. Pour the apple and ginger mixture in a glass with the lime juice. Stir well.
3. Top up with soda water then add the ice cubes, lime slice and sprig of mint.
4. Serve immediately.

Peach Mojito

1 tbsp mint syrup
2 shots tropical juice
1 tsp sugar
2 shots lime juice
2 handfuls ice cubes
2 peaches, cut into thin wedges
soda water

TO SERVE
sprig of mint
1 peach wedge

1. Mash the mint syrup, tropical juice and sugar together in a glass.
2. Add the lime juice, ice cubes and peach wedges.
3. Top up with soda water.
4. Serve garnished with a sprig of mint and a wedge of peach.

Pink Lemon Drop

3 ice cubes
2 shots lemon juice
2 shots lime juice
1 tsp sugar syrup
150 ml / 5 fl. oz pink lemonade

TO SERVE
1 lemon slice

1. Put the ice into the cocktail shaker.
2. Add the lemon juice, lime juice and sugar syrup over the ice in the shaker, then shake for 10 seconds.
3. Pour into a glass and top up with the pink lemonade.
4. Serve immediately with an added lemon slice.

SERVES: 1 | PREPARATION TIME: 5 MINS

Miss Margaret Rita

3 handfuls crushed ice
2 shots fresh lime juice
3 shots pineapple juice
a pinch of salt

TO SERVE
1 lime slice

1. Put two handfuls of crushed ice into the cocktail shaker.
2. Pour the lime juice and pineapple juice over the crushed ice in the shaker, then shake for 10 seconds.
3. Dip the rim of the margarita glass in water, then salt.
4. Pour the mixture into the glass and add another handful of crushed ice.
5. Serve garnished with a lime slice.

Strawberry Sling

1 handful strawberries, washed
7 ice cubes
2 shots of orange juice
soda water

TO SERVE
1 orange slice
sprig of mint

1. Process the strawberries through a juicer according to the manufacturer's instructions.
2. Meanwhile, put the ice cubes into the cocktail shaker.
3. Add the orange juice over the ice in the shaker, then shake for 10 seconds.
4. Pour into a glass and add the strawberry juice.
5. Top up the mocktail with soda water.
6. Serve with an orange slice and a sprig of mint.

SERVES: **1** | PREPARATION TIME: **5 MINS**

Tropical Hurricane

2 handfuls ice cubes

1 shot lime juice

1 shot lemon juice

2 shots passion fruit juice

2 shots pineapple juice, strained

1 shot grenadine

TO SERVE

2 strawberries, sliced

1 lemon, sliced

2 mint leaves

5 ice cubes

1. Put the ice cubes into the cocktail shaker.
2. Pour the lime juice, lemon juice, passion fruit juice, pineapple juice and grenadine over the ice cubes in the cocktail shaker, then shake for 20 seconds.
3. Strain into a glass or jar.
4. Add the sliced strawberries, lemon slices and mint leaves.
5. Serve immediately with more ice cubes.

SERVES: **1** | PREPARATION TIME: **5 MINS**

Mango Colada

2 handfuls mango chunks
2 handfuls crushed ice
5 shots pineapple juice
2 shots coconut cream
3 shots mango juice
3 shots tropical juice

TO SERVE
sprig of mint

1. Put the mango chunks and one handful of crushed ice in a blender and whizz for 20 seconds.
2. Put the other handful of crushed ice into the cocktail shaker.
3. Pour the blended mango, pineapple juice and coconut cream over the crushed ice in the shaker and shake for at least 30 seconds.
4. Pour into a glass and top up with the mango juice and tropical juice. Stir well with a cocktail mixer.
5. Serve garnished with a mint sprig.

Index

To Chris

With lo

from Dad + Mum

CW00321710

NO-BALLS AND
GOOGLIES

NO-BALLS AND GOOGLIES
A Cricket Companion

GEOFF TIBBALLS

MICHAEL O'MARA BOOKS LIMITED

First published in Great Britain in 2006 by
Michael O'Mara Books Limited
9 Lion Yard, Tremadoc Road
London sw4 7nq

A CIP catalogue record for this book is available
from the British Library

ISBN (10 digit): 1-84317-189-9
ISBN (13 digit): 978-1-84317-189-8

1 3 5 7 9 10 8 6 4 2

www.mombooks.com

Designed and typeset by Martin Bristow

Printed and bound in Finland by WS Bookwell, Juva

Introduction

It is more than a game, this cricket,
it somehow holds a mirror up to English society.

<small>SIR NEVILLE CARDUS</small>

THE ENGLISH SUMMER can be a bleak time for sports fans. The national football team either flatters to deceive in tournaments or doesn't even flatter at all; Henmania at Wimbledon always ends in tears, as does Colin Montgomerie's participation in any of the golfing majors. Going into 2005 it seemed the only sure bet for future success was that Ellen MacArthur would somewhere find a stretch of water she hadn't sailed before, even if it was a case of navigating the Diana Memorial Fountain in Hyde Park in record time. Then something truly remarkable happened: the England cricket team awoke from its slumbers to regain the Ashes for the first time in eighteen years. The manner of victory over the old enemy Australia, in what was arguably the most thrilling Ashes series ever, introduced a whole new generation of followers to the game. People whose only previous knowledge of cricket was that it was a game that took a long time to produce no result were suddenly talking about 'flippers' and 'sliders' and hailing 'Freddie' Flintoff as the new Messiah.

The resurgence of interest in cricket in this country is a matter for national rejoicing. For it is a quintessentially English game, one that has, from its very beginnings, attracted the humble blacksmith and the lord of the manor alike. What other pastime could unite Mick Jagger and John Major? Of course, at grass roots level, cricket's popularity has never waned. I spent much of my childhood following my father around the club grounds of south-east England. Like many a club player he was an all-rounder, generally batting at around number six – although occasionally elevated to opener if someone's car had broken down – and bowling economical medium pacers that 'did a bit'. Nobody, least of all him, I suspect, knew exactly what they did or how they came to do it. Apart from hoping that he would be out early so that I could gain some much-needed batting practice behind the pavilion, my principal job was to work the scoreboard, a task that involved nothing more technical than putting large numbered metal plates on to hooks. It was a blissful, stress-free existence, the only pressure coming from a fear of running out of certain numbers. A score of 66–6 with both batsmen on 6 was the stuff of nightmares. Meanwhile, my mother would sit in front of the pavilion, knitting for England. Unless it was a home game – in which case she would be on tea duty – she could have both sleeves finished by first change. It was a scene repeated among families up and down the land.

To this day, the mere mention of the word 'cricket' instantly conjures up an image of lazy summer afternoons, a village green, the reassuring sound of leather on willow, and the gentle ripple of applause. For all the appeal of the modern Twenty20 game with its instant gratification, it is an image that, in such uncertain times, we would do well to preserve.

No sport has a more fascinating background than cricket. Its lengthy history is rich in colourful characters, many of whose exploits are recounted within these pages. The rules themselves are a total mystery to the outsider, it has a language all of its own and there is a statistic to cover any eventuality. A cunning combination of subtlety, elegance and occasional brute force, it is a truly unique game, which, at its best, is aesthetically pleasing to the eye. Has there ever been a more glorious sight in sport than a perfectly executed cover drive by the likes of Tom Graveney or David Gower? Equally, is any sporting contest more compelling than Shane Warne trying to lure an obdurate batsman into an indiscretion? My hope is that this book will whet the appetite of those new to the game and provide nuggets of trivia and information to surprise even cricket's most dedicated followers. All statistics are correct up to 1 January 2006.

Finally, I would like to thank Helen Cumberbatch and the rest of the team at Michael O'Mara for making this project a true labour of love.

GEOFF TIBBALLS
Nottingham, 2006

A 'SIMPLE' EXPLANATION
OF THE GAME

YOU HAVE TWO SIDES: one out in the field and one in. Each man that's in the side that's in goes out, and when he's out he comes in, and the next man goes in until he's out. When they are all out, the side that's out comes in, and the side that's been in goes out and tries to get those coming in out. Sometimes you get men still in and not out. When a man goes out to go in, the men who are out try to get him out, and when he is out he goes in, and the next man goes out and goes in. There are also two men called umpires who stay out all the time and they decide when the men who are in are out. When both sides have been in and all the men except one have been out, and both sides have been out twice after all the men have been in, including those who are not out, that is the end of the game.

SOME EARLY REFERENCES
TO CRICKET

c.1550   Evidence of cricket being played at Guildford, Surrey.

1611   Two young men are fined for playing cricket on a Sunday at Sidlesham, Sussex.

1613   An assault with a 'cricket staffe' was reported at Wanborough, near Guildford, Surrey.

1624   Inquest on Jasper Vinall, who was accidentally killed with a cricket bat on Horsted Green, Sussex.

1629   Henry Cuffin, a curate from Ruckinge, Kent, appeared before the Archdeacon's Court for 'playing at Cricketts' immediately after divine service.

1648   A court case examined the death of Thomas Hatter, fatally injured by a cricket bat at Selsey, Sussex.

1658   A cricket ball was referred to in a book by Edward Phillips, nephew of poet John Milton.

1676   First reference to overseas cricket, by British residents in Aleppo, Syria.

1678   The first edition of Dr Adam Littleton's *Latin Dictionary* defines cricket as 'a game of stick and ball'.

1697   *The Foreign Post* wrote: 'A great match at Cricket was played in Sussex; there were eleven a side, and they played for fifty guineas apiece.'

1709   The first inter-county match took place: Kent v Surrey at Dartford.

1729   The earliest surviving bat was made, owned originally by John Chitty of Knaphill, Surrey. It now resides in the pavilion at the Oval.

1744   The first laws of cricket were drawn up.

1745   The first recorded women's cricket match took place at Gosden Common, near Guildford, Surrey.

1755   The first edition of Dr Samuel Johnson's *Dictionary* defines cricket as: 'A sport, at which the contenders drive a ball with sticks in opposition to each other.'

c.1767   Foundation of the Hambledon Club in Hampshire.

1769   The first recorded century – 107 by John Minshull for the Duke of Dorset's XI v Wrotham.

1771   The maximum width of the bat was established at 4.25 inches.

1776   The first known scorecards were used at Sevenoaks, Kent.

I ran for a catch
With the sun in my eyes, sir,
Being sure at a 'snatch'
I ran for a catch;
Now I wear a black patch
And a nose such a size, sir!
I ran for a catch
With the sun in my eyes, sir.

COULSON KERNAHAN

ORIGINS OF THE GAME

THE WORD 'CRICKET' derives from the diminutive of the Anglo-Saxon *cric*, meaning a staff or crutch. A manuscript in the Bodleian Library at Oxford contains a picture of one monk bowling a ball to another, who is about to strike it with a cric; other monks are 'in the field'. There are no wickets, but the batsman stands before a hole, and the aim of the game was either to get the ball into the hole or to catch it after it had been struck by the man with the cric.

The court accounts of 1300 refer to a game called 'creag' being played in Kent. This game, thought to be a forerunner of cricket, subsequently incurred the wrath of Edward III, who banned it, along with such pursuits as football and bowls, because at a time of war with France he wanted the archers of England to practise the bow and arrow without any other sporting distractions. More reliable evidence of the existence of cricket stems from 1598, when, in a dispute over a plot of land, John Derrick of Guildford described how fifty years earlier 'he and several of his fellows did runne and play there at cricket and other plaies'. This would indicate that cricket was played in the Guildford area around 1550.

Given the difficulty of seeing a hole in the ground, the following century a single stump was placed at each hole to point out the spot to bowlers and fielders. A tree stump was sometimes used, but because there weren't many trees on the downs of Sussex and Kent, where the game had its stronghold, a new target had to be found – the 'wicket-gate', through which passed flocks of sheep. This gate took the form of a small hurdle, consisting of two uprights known as stumps. The stumps were 12 inches high and set 24 inches apart. On

top of them was laid a crosspiece, known to this day in Australian pastures as a bail. This presented a superior target to a tree stump, as there could be no argument when the bail fell to the ground. The earliest bats were like cumbersome hockey sticks and were rounded at the end to deal with the ball bowled literally, as the word suggests, all along the ground. The score was kept by 'notching' runs with a knife on to a stick, a deeper groove being carved for every tenth run.

OLDEST
TEST MATCH PLAYERS

Years	Days	
52	165	WILFRED RHODES (England v West Indies, Kingston, 1929–30)
50	327	HERBERT IREMONGER (Australia v England, Sydney, 1932–3)
50	320	W. G. GRACE (England v Australia, Trent Bridge, 1899)
50	303	GEORGE GUNN (England v West Indies, Kingston, 1929–30)
49	139	JAMES SOUTHERTON (England v Australia, Melbourne, 1876–7)
47	302	MIRAN BUX (Pakistan v India, Peshawar, 1954–5)
47	249	JACK HOBBS (England v Australia, Oval, 1930)
47	87	FRANK WOOLLEY (England v Australia, Oval, 1934)
46	309	DON BLACKIE (Australia v England, Adelaide, 1928–9)
46	202	HERBERT STRUDWICK (England v Australia, Oval, 1926)
46	41	PATSY HENDREN (England v West Indies, Kingston, 1934–5)
45	304	ATHANASIOS TRAICOS (Zimbabwe v India, Delhi, 1992–3)
45	245	GUBBY ALLEN (England v West Indies, Kingston, 1947–8)
45	215	PERCY HOLMES (England v India, Lord's, 1932)
45	207	ARTHUR NOURSE (South Africa v England, Oval, 1924)
45	140	BRIAN CLOSE (England v West Indies, Old Trafford, 1976)

CRICKET ON THE SABBATH

IN 1622, a presentment (formal complaint) was made by parish authorities to the church hierarchy regarding two games of cricket played in Boxgrove churchyard, West Sussex, on Sundays 28 April and 5 May. The presentment read:

> I present Raphe West, Edward Hartley, Richard Slaughter, William Martin, Richard Martin junior, together with others in their company whose names I have no notice of, for playing at cricket in the churchyard on Sunday, the fifte of May, after sufficient warning given to the contrary, for three speciall reasons: first, for that it is contrary to the 7th article; secondly, for that they use to breake the church-windowes with the ball; and thirdly, for that a little childe had like to have her braynes beaten out with a cricket batt.
>
> And also I present Richard Martin senior and Thomas West the old churchwardens for defending and mayntayning them in it.
>
> Wee present Anthony Ward, servant to Mr Earle, our minister, and Edward Hartley, for playing at cricket in evening prayer tyme on Sunday the xxviijth of Aprill.

The accused appeared before the Consistory Court in Chichester Cathedral and, after publicly confessing their sins, each had to pay one shilling towards the court's expenses.

THE FIRST LAWS

THE EARLIEST KNOWN LAWS of cricket were laid down in 1744. They stipulated that the pitch be 22 yards long, that the distance between the bowling crease and the popping crease be 46 inches, that the wickets be 22 inches tall and 6 inches wide, and that the ball weigh between 5 and 6 ounces. These were amended in 1755, and further changes were introduced over the next 100 years or so.

1771 The maximum width of
the bat was set at 4.25
inches after Thomas White
of Reigate, in an unsporting
act, used a bat as wide as the
wicket against Hambledon.

1774 The lbw law was devised. William
Beldham, a member of the
influential Hambledon club, wrote:
'The Law for leg before wicket was
not made, nor much wanted, till Ring,
one of our best hitters, was shabby
enough to get his leg in the way and
take advantage of the bowlers, and
when Tom Taylor, another of the best
hitters, did the same, the bowlers
found themselves beaten and the law
was passed.'

1775 The third stump was added to the
wicket after Hambledon's John Small
won a game single-handed because
opposing bowlers repeatedly beat his defence only to see the
ball fly between the stumps without disturbing them.

1788 The Marylebone Cricket Club published a set of Laws of
Cricket, which were adopted by other clubs across England.
The MCC remains the custodian of the Laws of Cricket to
the present day.

1821 The distance between the bowling and popping creases was
increased from 46 to 48 inches.

1838 The size of a cricket ball was codified for the first time, being
a circumference between 9 and 9.25 inches.

1889 Sides were allowed to declare an innings closed.

Extracts from *A Code of Laws of Cricket*, First Published in 1755

Laws for the Bowler

If he delivers ye Ball with his hinder foot over ye Crease ye Umpire shall call No Ball though he be struck or ye Player is bowled out, which he shall do without being asked and no Person shall have any right to ask him.

Laws for the Umpires

To allow two minutes for each Man to come in when one is out and ten minutes between each Hand. To mark ye Ball that it may not be changed. They are sole judges of all Outs and Ins, of all Fair and Unfair play or frivolous delays, of all hurts whether real or pretended,

and are discretionally to allow what time they think proper before ye Game goes on again. In case of a real hurt to a Striker they are to allow another to come in & ye Person hurt to come in again. But are not to allow a fresh Man to play on either Side on any Account. They are sole judges of all hindrances, crossing ye Players in running & standing unfair to strike & in case of hindrance may order a notch to be scored. They are not to order any Man out *unless appealed to* by any one of ye Players. These Laws are to ye Umpires jointly. Each Umpire is ye sole judge of all Nips and Catches, Ins and Outs, good or bad Runs at his own Wicket & his determination shall be absolute & he shall not be changed for another Umpire without ye consent of both sides. When ye 4 Balls are bowled, he is to call Over. When both Umpires shall call Play, three times, 'tis at ye peril of giving ye Game from them that refuse to Play.

and

3. When ye Ball has been in hand by one of ye Keepers or Stoppers and ye Player has been at home, He may go where he pleases till ye next ball is bowled. If either of ye Strikers is cross'd in his running ground designedly, which design must be determined by ye Umpires, ye Umpires may order that Notch to be scored.

Most Runs
in Test Matches

		Runs	Average
1.	BRIAN LARA (West Indies)	11,204	53.86
2.	ALLAN BORDER (Australia)	11,174	50.56
3.	STEVE WAUGH (Australia)	10,927	51.06
4.	SACHIN TENDULKAR (India)	10,323	56.71
5.	SUNIL GAVASKAR (India)	10,122	51.12
6.	GRAHAM GOOCH (England)	8,900	42.58
7.	JAVED MIANDAD (Pakistan)	8,832	52.57
8.	VIV RICHARDS (West Indies)	8,540	50.23
9.	ALEC STEWART (England)	8,463	39.54
10.	DAVID GOWER (England)	8,231	44.25
11.	GEOFFREY BOYCOTT (England)	8,114	47.72
12.	INZAMAM-UL-HAQ (Pakistan)	8,052	51.61
13.	GARY SOBERS (West Indies)	8,032	57.78
14.	MARK WAUGH (Australia)	8,029	41.81
15.	RAHUL DRAVID (India)	8,003	57.16
16.	RICKY PONTING (Australia)	7,990	56.26
17.	MIKE ATHERTON (England)	7,728	37.69
18.	COLIN COWDREY (England)	7,624	44.06
19.	GORDON GREENIDGE (West Indies)	7,558	44.72
20.	MARK TAYLOR (Australia)	7,525	43.49
21.	CLIVE LLOYD (West Indies)	7,515	46.67
22.	DESMOND HAYNES (West Indies)	7,487	42.29
23.	DAVID BOON (Australia)	7,422	43.65
24.	JACQUES KALLIS (South Africa)	7,420	57.07
25.	GARY KIRSTEN (South Africa)	7,289	45.27
26.	WALLY HAMMOND (England)	7,249	58.45
27.	JUSTIN LANGER (Australia)	7,226	46.02
28.	GREG CHAPPELL (Australia)	7,110	53.86
29.	DONALD BRADMAN (Australia)	6,996	99.94
30.	LEN HUTTON (England)	6,971	56.67

OF BAT AND BALL

THE CRICKET-BAT WILLOW (*Salix alba* var. 'Caerulea') is grown as a specialist timber crop in Britain, mainly for the production of cricket bats, but also for other instances where a tough, lightweight, splinter-resistant wood is required (it was formerly much in demand for the manufacture of artificial limbs). The tree's origin is unknown, but it may be a hybrid of white willow (*Salix alba*) and crack willow (*Salix fragilis*). Specialist cricket-bat makers buy timber for bats many years before it is ready for harvesting.

The earliest reference to a cricket ball was in *The Mysteries of Love and Eloquence* by Edward Phillips in 1658. A character exclaims: 'Would my eyes had been beat out of my head with a cricket-ball, the day before I saw thee!' Today's cricket balls are made from the same materials as those used in the eighteenth century: cork and latex rubber on the inside, with leather on the outside.

Sir Donald Bradman
Would have been a very glad man
If his Test average had been .06 more
Than 99.94.

T. N. E. SMITH

Most Wickets in Test Matches

	Wickets	Average
Shane Warne (Australia)	657	24.99
Muttiah Muralitharan (Sri Lanka)	584	22.47
Glenn McGrath (Australia)	539	21.44
Courtney Walsh (West Indies)	519	24.44
Anil Kumble (India)	485	27.98
Kapil Dev (India)	434	29.64
Richard Hadlee (New Zealand)	431	22.29
Wasim Akram (Pakistan)	414	23.62
Curtly Ambrose (West Indies)	405	20.99
Shaun Pollock (South Africa)	384	22.39
Ian Botham (England)	383	28.40
Malcolm Marshall (West Indies)	376	20.94
Waqar Younis (Pakistan)	373	23.56
Imran Khan (Pakistan)	362	22.81
Dennis Lillee (Australia)	355	23.92
Allan Donald (South Africa)	330	22.25
Bob Willis (England)	325	25.20
Lance Gibbs (West Indies)	309	29.09
Fred Trueman (England)	307	21.57
Chaminda Vaas (Sri Lanka)	301	28.81
Derek Underwood (England)	297	25.83
Craig McDermott (Australia)	291	28.63
Bishen Bedi (India)	266	28.71
Joel Garner (West Indies)	259	20.97
Brian Statham (England)	252	24.84
Jason Gillespie (Australia)	251	26.61
Michael Holding (West Indies)	249	23.68
Richie Benaud (Australia)	248	27.03
Graham McKenzie (Australia)	246	29.78
Bhagwat Chandrasekhar (India)	242	29.74

THE HAMBLEDON CLUB

ALTHOUGH historical evidence suggests that the game was first played in the Weald around Kent and Sussex, it is the Hambledon Club of Hampshire that is generally perceived as cricket's spiritual home. Founded around 1767, Hambledon was the leading club in England for some thirty years, regularly drawing crowds of 20,000 to its matches on Broad Halfpenny Down. An indication of its might was that in 1777, Hambledon scored 403 against All England. Key players included the captain Richard Nyren, bowler David Harris, and master batsman John Small, reputedly the first man to abandon the old curved bat in favour of a straight blade. Hambledon's influence was ended by the formation of the Marylebone Cricket Club, which attracted major players to London.

Here lies, bowl'd out by Death's unerring ball,
A cricketer renowned, by name John Small;
But though his name was small, yet great was his fame,
For nobly did he play the 'noble game'.
His life was like his innings – long and good;
Full ninety summers had Death withstood,
At length the ninetieth winter came – when (Fate
Not leaving him one solitary mate)
This last of Hambledonians, old John Small,
Gave up his bat and ball – his leather, wax and all.

PIERCE EGAN

BOWLING CHANGES

BY THE START of the nineteenth century the finest batsmen had mastered underarm bowling. Lord Frederick Beauclerk, whose confidence was such that he used to hang his gold watch from the bails, averaged 61 in 1803. It was time for the country's bowlers to try something new. Around 1790 Hambledon's Thomas Walker had attempted to bowl round-arm (i.e. his bowling arm level with his shoulder), but because he had been verbally abused for doing so he quickly returned to more conventional methods. Over in Kent, John Willes was enjoying batting practice with his sister Christina in a barn near their Canterbury home. Struggling to deliver the ball underarm owing to the voluminous skirt she was wearing, Christina instead began bowling round-arm to him. Willes immediately recognized the possibilities, and in 1807 he employed round-arm

while bowling for Kent against All England. But the new action was not recognized officially and, in 1822, when Willes bowled round-arm at the haughty Beauclerk in an MCC v Kent match, his Lordship protested against the 'illegal' bowling. Willes is reported to have thrown down the ball in disgust, ridden out of Lord's and never played in a first-class game again. Another Kent amateur George Knight took up Willes's crusade, however, and in 1835, the law was finally amended to allow the bowler's hand to be raised as high as the shoulder.

The change created a new illegal phenomenon: that of the high bowler – one whose arm was raised above his shoulder in an overarm fashion. Matters came to a head on 26 August 1862, when Surrey entertained England at the Oval. Kent left-armer Edgar Willsher was called for six no-balls in succession by umpire John Lillywhite, whereupon Willsher stormed off the field, followed by the rest of the England team. The *Daily Telegraph* reported: 'On inquiry, we learnt that, on bowling his second over, Willsher was cautioned by John Lillywhite that he was getting high in delivery, and that he should "no-ball" him if he continued to so deliver the balls.' In order that the match could be completed, Lillywhite graciously offered to step down and Willsher, permitted to bowl high and unchecked by the new umpire, went on to take six wickets. The incident prompted much newspaper discussion, and two years later cricket's lawmakers voted 27–20 in favour of removing the restrictions on overarm bowling.

WITH DIGNITY AND CALM

With dignity and calm, but debonair,
He left the awed pavilion, head in air,
His gear and garments faultlessly assembled.
His shirt was silken, pen could never trace
The beauty of his trousers' matchless grace
And as he walked to his appointed place,
The bowlers trembled.
The wicket reached, he eyed the umpires hard,
With most elaborate caution took his guard,
Made a hole, then ground his heel within it.
While the field grew tremulous and pale
He banged it, he poked it, he measured it to scale,
And then he went and scratched it with a bail
For quite a minute.
This done, the pitch he viewed with care,
A speck of dust removing here and there;
Prodding and sweeping, hammering and patting,
The wicketkeeper looking on aghast.
He made the buckles of his leg-guards fast,
Adjusted his gloves, and seemed disposed at last
To think of batting.
Not yet. Unblushingly he now began
To note the fielders, studying every man
With keen regard, as if each only mattered.
But in the end he took his stance, his brow
Showed keen resolve. He faced the bowler, now.
There came a horrid row –
His stumps were scattered.

With dignity he made his way
Back to the dumb pavilion.
I must say his mien was proud, his gait was firm and steady,
And as upon the scoring-board they stuck,
With callous haste, a large and hideous duck,
He said, in high clear accent, 'What putrid luck,
I wasn't ready.'

ANONYMOUS

THE DERIVATION OF
SOME CRICKETING TERMS

BEAMER: This wild and dangerous full toss is said to have been
patented by a Cambridge University fast bowler who, irked by
the placid pitches at his home ground of Fenners, elected to
upset the complacency of opposing batsmen by unleashing a
threat to their personal safety. At Fenners it was very difficult to
detect the ball in flight, since the ball came at the batsmen out
of a dark background of trees.

BOSIE: An Australian term for the googly, named after its English inventor B. J. T. Bosanquet. In 1897 he was playing a game with a tennis ball, called 'Twisti-Twosti'. 'The object,' he explained, 'was to bounce the ball so that your opponent sitting opposite could not catch it. It soon occurred to me that if one could pitch a ball which broke in a certain direction and with more or less the same delivery make the next ball go in the opposite direction, one would mystify one's opponent.' He then perfected the art with a cricket ball and used it to great effect on the 1904–5 tour to Australia.

CHINAMAN: Some cricket historians claim that this term originated from the 1929–30 series between England and the West Indies. The West Indies team included Ellis Achong, a left-arm wrist-spinner of Chinese descent, who bowled a ball that deceived Walter Robins and led to his stumping. The story goes that on returning to the dressing-room, Robins was heard to exclaim, 'Fancy getting out to a bloody Chinaman!' Another possibility is that the term derives from the politically incorrect connotations of deviousness associated in old-fashioned English eyes with the words 'Chinese' and 'Chinaman'.

CREASE: This term comes from the basic meaning of a crease, which is 'a furrow in the surface', because it was originally cut in the turf. This method of marking continued until 1865, when painted lines were introduced.

FERRET: A terrible batsman, so poor that, as in pest control, he is sent in after the rabbits.

GOOGLY: When it first appeared, this delivery mystified batsmen so much that it made their eyes 'goggle'.

HAT-TRICK: This term originates from a mid-nineteenth-century custom whereby any bowler who took three wickets in three balls was presented with a hat. Surrey's H. H. Stephenson was the first to be awarded a hat, after performing the feat for the All England XI against Hallam in September 1858.

MAIDEN OVER: Before becoming part of the vocabulary of cricket, the word 'maiden' had long been used in English to mean 'unproductive'. Hence, in cricket, a maiden over is an unproductive one, from which no runs are scored.

NELSON: Denoting the score 111, the use of this word stems from the misconception that Admiral Nelson lost one arm, one eye and one leg in battle.

POPPING CREASE: Under the early rules of cricket, on completion of a 'notch' or run, the batsman had to place his bat in a popping hole that was cut in the turf. In order to get the batsman out, the wicketkeeper had to put the ball in this hole before the batsman could reach it with his bat. However, this rule led to serious hand injuries and was later superseded by the batsman having to touch a stick held by the umpire. Eventually the popping hole was represented symbolically by a popping crease for the purposes of signifying the completion of a run.

UMPIRE: The word stems from the old French 'nompere', from 'non per' which means 'not equal', indicating an 'odd man' or third party called in to adjudicate between two contestants.

YORKER: Tom Emmett, who played for Yorkshire in the nineteenth century, was so successful at bowling this type of ball (a full-length delivery pitched on the popping crease in the hope that it will squeeze under the bat) that teammate George Ulyett reportedly said, 'See the', Tom lad, if thou goes on bowling them sort of balls, aa'll have to call them Yorkers.'

MASTER OF THE SWEEP

ON 15 AUGUST 1877, a Gloucestershire XI with broomsticks played Eleven of Cheltenham with bats. Dr E. M. Grace, batting with a broomstick, made 103 in the Gloucestershire total of 290.

Hat-tricks in Test Matches

FRED SPOFFORTH (Australia v England, Melbourne, 1879)

BILLY BATES (England v Australia, Melbourne, 1883)

JOHNNY BRIGGS (England v Australia, Sydney, 1892)

GEORGE LOHMANN (England v South Africa, Port Elizabeth, 1896)

JACK HEARNE (England v Australia, Headingley, 1899)

HUGH TRUMBLE (Australia v England, Melbourne, 1902)

HUGH TRUMBLE (Australia v England, Melbourne, 1904)

JIMMY MATTHEWS (Australia v South Africa first innings, Old Trafford, 1912)

JIMMY MATTHEWS (Australia v South Africa second innings, Old Trafford, 1912)

MAURICE ALLOM (England v New Zealand, Christchurch, 1930)

TOM GODDARD (England v South Africa, Johannesburg, 1938)

PETER LOADER (England v West Indies, Headingley, 1957)

LINDSAY KLINE (Australia v South Africa, Cape Town, 1958)

WES HALL (West Indies v Pakistan, Lahore, 1959)

GEOFF GRIFFIN (South Africa v England, Lord's, 1960)

LANCE GIBBS (West Indies v Australia, Adelaide, 1961)

PETER PETHERICK (New Zealand v Pakistan, Lahore, 1976)

COURTNEY WALSH (West Indies v Australia, Brisbane, 1988)

MERV HUGHES (Australia v West Indies, Perth, 1988)

DAMIEN FLEMING (Australia v Pakistan, Rawalpindi, 1994)

SHANE WARNE (Australia v England, Melbourne, 1994)

Dominic Cork (England v West Indies, Old Trafford, 1995)

DARREN GOUGH (England v Australia, Sydney, 1999)

WASIM AKRAM (Pakistan v Sri Lanka, Lahore, 1999)

WASIM AKRAM (Pakistan v Sri Lanka, Dhaka, 1999)

NUWAN ZOYSA (Sri Lanka v Zimbabwe, Harare, 1999)

ABDUR RAZZAQ (Pakistan v Sri Lanka, Galle, 2000)

GLENN MCGRATH (Australia v West Indies, Perth, 2000)

HARBHAJAN SINGH (India v Australia, Calcutta, 2001)
MOHAMMAD SAMI (Pakistan v Sri Lanka, Lahore, 2002)
JERMAINE LAWSON (West Indies v Australia, Bridgetown, 2003)
ALOK KAPALI (Bangladesh v Pakistan, Peshawar, 2003)
ANDY BLIGNAUT (Zimbabwe v Bangladesh, Harare, 2004)
MATTHEW HOGGARD (England v West Indies, Barbados, 2004)
JAMES FRANKLIN (New Zealand v Bangladesh, Dhaka, 2004)

DOG DAY AFTERNOON

ON 21 MAY 1827, one of the most unorthodox games in the history of cricket took place on Harefield Common, near Rickmansworth, when a local farmer, Francis Trumper, and his sheepdog succeeded in defeating 'two gentlemen of Middlesex'. Apparently, the day was won by the dog's agility in the field as, according to *The Times*, spectators from Uxbridge and surrounding villages were 'much astonished at the dog's dexterity'. *The Times* continued: 'The dog always stood near his master when he was going to bowl, and the moment the ball was hit he kept his eye upon it, and started off after it with speed; and, on his master running up to the wicket, the dog would carry the ball in his mouth and put it into his master's hand with such wonderful quickness that the gentlemen found it very difficult to get a run even from a very long hit.'

CURIOUS INTERRUPTIONS TO PLAY

- A Second XI match between Derbyshire and Leicester-shire was held up in June 2005 by a rampaging bull. The animal jumped the fence from a neighbouring field in the Staffordshire village of Dunstall and chased players and spectators for twenty minutes.

- In April 1997, bad flight stopped play in Lincolnshire after a fielder in the Horncastle–Bardney game was hit on the head by a wayward hang-glider.

- A fish once stopped play in Sri Lanka. The two-foot specimen landed in the middle of the pitch, dropped by a sea eagle that was being harassed by crows.

- A swarm of bees stopped play for several minutes at Sophia Gardens, Cardiff, in June 2005. Glamorgan fielders and visiting Kent batsmen fell flat on the ground to avoid being stung.

- Play in the match between Launceston and Old Suttonians in August 1984 had to be halted on four separate occasions after a herd of camels strayed on to the pitch from a nearby circus.

- Play in a match at Queen's Park Savannah, Trinidad, was stopped for several minutes after it was discovered that over-zealous police officers had slapped parking tickets on the cars of players and match officials.

- Play was twice held up during the Lancashire–Sussex match at Lytham St Anne's in 1995 when excerpts from a Holy Communion service at nearby St Cuthbert's Church were mysteriously broadcast via the ground's public address system.

- On 10 August 1967, the scorebook of Aden-based Venturers CC recorded: 'Play delayed ten minutes by mortar attack.'

- Umpire Dickie Bird took the players off the pitch in the 1995 Old Trafford Test between England and the West Indies because the light was too bright! The sun was shining on some adjacent greenhouses and reflecting on to the stands, as a result of which slip fielders and batsmen were unable to see the ball. Officials had to cover the greenhouses with black sheeting.

- The First Test between Young Sri Lanka and Young England in 1987 was stopped when a large iguana crept across the square at the Colombo Cricket Club ground.

- A 1998 game between Dorchester Third XI and the Parley Montys from Wimborne was held up when an irate wife drove her car on to the pitch. Jennifer Christian then hurled her car keys at the man fielding in the gully before running off, leaving their two children in the vehicle. Husband Eric drove off after her and played no further part in the match. The altercation is believed to have stemmed from a promise he made to look after the children that afternoon.

- A 1995 Winchester Evening League game between the fire brigade and the local rugby club was held up while the firemen formed a human chain to rescue an eleven-year-old boy who had got stuck in a tree.

- In 1892, a runaway horse and cart halted proceedings during the MCC–Yorkshire fixture at Scarborough.

- The final Test at Durban on England's 1922–3 tour of South Africa was interrupted by the appearance of a pile of small green frogs on the wicket. The stray animals were loaded into two buckets and moved to safer pastures.

- When South African Daryll Cullinan hit a six for Border against Boland in February 1995, the ball landed in a frying pan containing hot calamari. Although officials managed to remove the ball from the pan, play was delayed for ten minutes until the ball had cooled down sufficiently for the coating of grease to be removed.

- In July 2003, play at the Glamorgan v Somerset County Championship match at Cardiff was stopped for several minutes when around 200 seagulls invaded the pitch shortly after tea.

- Play in a match between Royston and Cambridge Victoria in 1890 was stopped while a stoat ran across the pitch.

- An exploding gas cylinder inside a pitch-side drinks dispenser held up play for ten minutes during the second Test between Pakistan and England at Faisalabad in November 2005.

- A 1982 fixture between Hampshire rivals Curdridge and Medstead was temporarily halted when a hot-air balloon promoting a local burger bar ran out of fuel and came down to earth between the stumps.

- Eight male streakers, thought to have been attending a stag party, stopped play in the Pembrokeshire League match between Neyland and Lawrenny in 1996.

- During a Notts v India match at Trent Bridge in 1974, play was stopped by parachutists who landed near the pitch when aiming for the nearby River Trent.

- In 1995, *Wisden* reported that a match at Boddington, Gloucestershire, had to be abandoned because the pitch was engulfed by smoke billowing from the nearby Companion's Rest animal crematorium.

DISTANT SHORES

ALTHOUGH THE APPEAL of cricket would eventually extend way beyond the boundaries of England, the initial step towards spreading the gospel was tentative to say the least. The first overseas touring team was organized in 1789, when the British government arranged for a team to play in Paris shortly after the start of the French Revolution as a goodwill gesture towards the newly formed National Assembly. The players got as far as Dover, where they met the British Ambassador to France fleeing in the opposite direction following renewed violence in Paris. Wisely, the tour was abandoned on the spot.

It was another seventy years before an English cricket XI finally made an overseas tour – the venue, somewhat surprisingly in view of subsequent sporting history, being the United States. Yet cricket had been popular in the eastern regions of both the US and Canada since the 1830s, and what is believed to be the oldest international sporting fixture in the world was the cricket match between Canada and the US in 1844 – more than thirty years before the start of the England–Australia series. The 1844 international originated from a hoax. A person calling himself Mr Phillpotts visited New York in 1840 and arranged for the city's St George's Club to travel to Canada for a match against Toronto CC, but when the New Yorkers arrived, nobody in Toronto knew anything about the fixture. Not wishing to appear ungracious hosts, the Canadians hastily assembled a side but lost by ten wickets. In 1843, Toronto played the return match in New York and the following year's encounter (essentially between the same clubs with a few reinforcements) was billed as United States v Canada.

By the time of the pioneering England tour of 1859, American cricket had spread to Philadelphia, where the standard was certainly the equal of Australia. The tour was the brainchild of W. P. Pickering, an Old Etonian who had emigrated to Canada, and after a Mr Waller of New York had guaranteed £500 for two matches in New Jersey and Philadelphia, twelve of the finest professional cricketers in the land set off from Liverpool on 7 September aboard the steamer *Nova Scotia*. The playing party comprised Tom Lockyer, Julius Caesar, H. H. Stephenson and William Caffyn of Surrey; George Parr (captain), Jeremy Grundy and John Jackson of Nottinghamshire; John Wisden and John Lillywhite of Sussex; and Tom Hayward, Alfred Diver and Robert Carpenter of Cambridgeshire. The players travelled over 7,000 miles in two months to play five matches, all of which they won. Although the tour was hailed as a success, the cold October weather restricted attendances in the final match, where it was reported that the fielders wore gloves and overcoats! The tour could quite conceivably

have led to Test matches between England and the United States, but two years later the American Civil War broke out and baseball became the national sport instead.

Prior to the Civil War, cricket was an established game while baseball was largely confined to students and children, but in the harsh days of war it was easier to find a patch of rough ground for baseball than the decent pitch needed to play cricket. So the England tour organizers turned their gaze to Australia instead, and cricket in the US went into decline, although as late as 1896 an Australian team visited Philadelphia and played three matches on level terms. And when Philadelphia toured England in 1908, their swing bowler Bart King topped the first-class English bowling

averages. The game's popularity blossomed in Canada, however, and in 1867 the country's first Prime Minister, Sir John A. Macdonald, declared cricket to be Canada's national sport.

Cricket was first reported as being played in Australia in 1804, on Philip's Common, an area of scrubland in Sydney. The *Sydney Gazette and New South Wales Advertiser* for 8 January revealed: 'The late intense weather has been very favourable to the amateurs of cricket who scarce have lost a day for the past month.' Cricket soon spread across the Tasman Sea, and in his diary entry for 23 December 1835, Charles Darwin, on the voyage of HMS *Beagle*, wrote that when his party arrived at Waiwata, New Zealand, he saw young Maori farm workers playing cricket on a farm run by British missionaries.

The first full tour of England by an overseas team took place in 1868. A party of fourteen Australian Aborigines, captained by Charles Lawrence, played an exhausting forty-seven matches, winning fourteen, losing fourteen, and drawing the remainder. In 1877, James Lillywhite led the first England team to tour Australia, stopping off first in New Zealand, where Surrey wicketkeeper Edward

Pooley was thrown into a jail after a gambling row had escalated into a brawl. By the time he stood trial, his depleted teammates (Pooley was the only wicketkeeper in the party) had travelled to Melbourne and lost the first Test by 45 runs. Two years later it was the Australians' turn to disgrace themselves, the Sydney crowd rioting and attacking England captain Lord Harris after local hero Billy Murdoch was adjudged run out.

By then, the British navy had helped spread cricket far and wide – to such locations as Singapore, Hong Kong, South Africa, Buenos Aires, Fiji, Egypt, Gibraltar, and Malta. In 1861, Prince Albert, second son of Queen Victoria, visited Barbados as a midshipman and spent much of one day playing cricket. The game was introduced to Samoa in 1884 and became so popular – with matches lasting weeks on end – that work was neglected and the King had to issue a proclamation to put a stop to his subjects' cricketing excesses:

THE LAW REGARDING CRICKET

To All The Districts of Samoa, Notice

1. It is strictly prohibited for a village to travel and play cricket with another village.
2. It is strictly prohibited for two villages to play cricket together.
3. It is also prohibited for a village to play cricket among themselves.

    Should any village or district fail to keep this law in any respect, they will be fined a sum not exceeding forty-five dollars, or in default be sent to jail for three months with hard labour.

MALIETOA, THE KING OF SAMOA
Residence of the King, Apia
June 20, 1890

Bombay was the birthplace of Indian cricket. The native Parsees adopted the strange English game and played the Old Etonians in the late eighteenth century. While the British brought their own top-of-the-range equipment, the Parsees were reduced to playing with cast-offs, as a result of which they batted with pieces of log or planks desperately held together by string. Despite these shortcomings, however, the Parsees embraced the game, and by the second half of the nineteenth century cricket was flourishing on the subcontinent. As a leading Indian patriot once remarked: 'The finest legacies left us by British Rule are the English language and, even more precious, the game of cricket.'

THE RABBIT

His record, take it all in all,
Was not a very great one:
He seldom hit a crooked ball
And never stopped a straight one.

ANONYMOUS

LOST IN TRANSLATION

IN JULY 1993, an English touring team called the Explorers played what is thought to be the first proper cricket match in Moscow since the Bolshevik Revolution. Their opponents were the MCC – the recently formed Moscow Cricket Club. However, due to a breakdown in communications, the pitch was originally laid out for a croquet match and broom-handles had to be used for stumps because the man responsible for the tourists' kit had been stopped at Heathrow after forgetting to obtain a visa.

BIRTH OF THE ASHES

THE CONCEPT OF THE ASHES originates from a mock obituary published shortly after England's first ever defeat to Australia on English soil in August 1882, when the demon bowling of Fred Spofforth (14 for 90) gave Australia a seven-run victory. Spofforth's last eleven overs included ten maidens and were bowled for two runs and four wickets as England, chasing a target of just 85 to win, crumbled to 77 all out. The latter stages were so tense that one English spectator – Epsom stockbroker Arthur Courcy – is said to have chewed through the handle of his brother-in-law's umbrella. The obituary, published in the *Sporting Times* of 2 September 1882, read:

In Affectionate Remembrance

OF

ENGLISH CRICKET

WHICH DIED AT THE OVAL

on

29th August, 1882,

Deeply lamented by a large circle of sorrowing
friends and acquaintances

R.I.P.

---

*N.B. – The body will be cremated
and the ashes taken to Australia.*

A few months later, an England team led by the Hon. Ivo Bligh went to Australia and regained the Ashes by beating the home side in a three-match series. To mark this achievement, some British ladies presented Bligh with a small urn containing the ashes of a set of bails that they had burned. The urn was kept by Bligh until his death in 1927, when it was bequeathed to the MCC. The Ashes always remain at Lord's, regardless of whether England or Australia wins the series. In any case, the title only changes hands if the current holders lose the series.

NATIONS'
FIRST TEST MATCHES

1877 England (v Australia) at Melbourne
1877 Australia (v England) at Melbourne
1889 South Africa (v England) at Port Elizabeth
1928 West Indies (v England) at Lord's
1930 New Zealand (v England) at Lord's
1932 India (v England) at Lord's
1952 Pakistan (v India) at Delhi
1982 Sri Lanka (v England) at Colombo
1992 Zimbabwe (v India) at Harare
2000 Bangladesh (v India) at Dhaka

AN ASHES MISCELLANY

- On 75–0 in reply to England's 145 in the final Test at the Oval in 1896, Australia seemed to be in a strong position until Frank Iredale was run out going for a fifth run. Australia promptly collapsed to 119 all out and ended up losing the match by 66 runs and the series 2–1.

- Australia's Clem Hill scored 99, 98 and 97 in successive Test innings in the 1901–2 Ashes series.

- As rain had reduced the 1921 Old Trafford Test to a two-day game, with the home side's score at over 300, the England captain – the Hon. Lionel Tennyson – went on to the field at 5.50 p.m. and called the players in. Batsmen Ernest Tyldesley and Percy Fender left the field, but Australian captain Warwick Armstrong stayed put, sitting near the stumps where he had been bowling. He then reminded the umpires that the law, amended in 1914, stipulated that a declaration in the event of a lost day could not be made later than an hour and forty minutes before close of play. Consequently, when play resumed twenty minutes later, England were still batting. Compounding their error, the umpires allowed Armstrong to bowl the first over after the resumption, meaning that the captain had bowled two in succession.

- Faced with a first-innings deficit of 304, England looked like making a fight of the second Test at Lord's in 1930 with

Percy Chapman unbeaten on 121. Then a bluebottle suddenly flew into his mouth and Chapman was still choking on the insect when he was caught behind. Australia went on to win by seven wickets.

- In the third Test of the 1930 series, Don Bradman scored over 300 runs in a day. He came in at 11.38 a.m. after Archie Jackson was dismissed in the second over. By lunch Bradman had made 105 (out of Australia's total of 136–1), by tea he had advanced to 220, and by close of play he had reached 309. When he was finally out the next day, his 334 runs had come from 436 balls and included 46 fours but no sixes. Interestingly, in his entire Test career, Bradman hit only six sixes, compared with 618 fours and two fives.

- When Maurice Leyland scored 187 in the 1938 Oval Test, he became the first Englishman to score centuries in his first and last innings against Australia. Nine years earlier he had made 137 in the fifth Test at Melbourne.

- As Ricky Ponting can testify, putting the opposition in to bat can be a dangerous tactic. At Brisbane in 1954, Len Hutton opted to field and could only watch in frustration as Australia built up an impressive 601–8 on their way to a comfortable innings victory.

- Fred Trueman became the first bowler to take 300 Test wickets when he had Neil Hawke caught at slip by Colin Cowdrey at the Oval in 1964.

- Making his way out to bat on his Test debut, at Lord's in 1975, England's David Steele descended one flight of steps too many and finished up in the pavilion toilets.

- At Trent Bridge in 1977 local hero Derek Randall had made twelve runs when Geoffrey Boycott called him for a tight single. Randall was duly run out by Jeff Thomson's throw to

wicketkeeper Rod Marsh, as a result of which Boycott was loudly booed by the home supporters. Though Boycott went on to make a century, he reckons the Nottingham public never forgave him.

- During the first Test at Perth in 1979, Dennis Lillee strode to the crease with an aluminium bat, and was ordered to change it for a more conventional appliance.

- Merv Hughes's vitriolic sledging of Graeme Hick during the 1989 series prompted umpire Dickie Bird to intervene and ask concernedly: 'Mervyn, Mervyn, those are terrible things to say. What has that nice Mr Hick ever done to you?'

- Named 'the ball of the century', Shane Warne's first delivery in Test cricket in England was to Mike Gatting at Old Trafford on 4 June 1993. The ball drifted lazily wide of leg stump, scarcely enough to maintain the batsman's interest, then spat back a yard or two and clipped the top of the bails off. Graham Gooch said of Gatting's stunned expression as he walked off: 'He looked as though someone had just nicked his lunch.' Australia went on to win the match by 179 runs and the series 4–1, *Wisden* noting that 'never, perhaps, has one delivery cast so long a shadow over a game, or a series.'

- In 1995, at Perth, Steve Waugh was left stranded on 99 not out after last man Craig McDermott was deemed run out. The injured McDermott was using a runner – Steve Waugh's twin, Mark – who, in trying to help his brother reach a century, failed to reach the crease after being sent back by his cautious sibling.

- In the final Test at Sydney in 1999, Darren Gough took three wickets in successive balls to become the first Englishman to take a hat-trick in an Ashes Test in the twentieth century.

- On the 2002–3 tour Down Under, an Aussie fan called out to Phil Tufnell: 'Hey Tufnell, can I borrow your brain. I'm building an idiot.'

TEN CLOSE ASHES FINISHES

Second Test, Edgbaston, 2005

Set a ground record 282 to win, Australia nearly pulled off a remarkable victory. Even after Shane Warne had trodden on his wicket playing back to man-of-the-match Andrew Flintoff, Brett Lee and Michael Kasprowicz added a nail-biting 59 for the last wicket, before Kasprowicz gloved a Steve Harmison bouncer down the leg side to wicketkeeper Geraint Jones to give England victory by just two runs. To add to the drama, TV replays suggested that Kasprowicz should not have been given out, as he had taken his lower hand off the bat before the ball hit the glove.

Fourth Test, Old Trafford, 1902

This was the Test known ironically as 'Tate's match'. Leading by 37 runs after the first innings – thanks largely to a swashbuckling century from Victor Trumper – Australia were reeling at 16–3 in their second innings when England fielder Fred Tate dropped Joe Darling at deep square leg. Darling went on to make a valuable 37 as Australia scrambled to 84 all out. England were then bowled out for 120 and ended up losing by three runs, with the unfortunate Tate the last man out. It was to be his only Test.

Third Test, Sydney, 1885

With England leading 2–0 in the series, Australia's hopes looked bleak when they were bowled out for 181, Wilfred Flowers taking 5 for 46. But England fared even worse, Flowers top-scoring with 24

as they struggled to 133. After dismissing Australia for 165 in their second innings, England needed 207 to win but a hailstorm enlivened the pitch, enabling Aussie Fred Spofforth to run riot, taking 6 for 60. Even so, Flowers was still bravely hanging on after scoring 56, until a remarkable catch at point by Edwin Evans ended his courageous innings and saw Australia home by just six runs.

Oval Test, 1882

The game that inspired the whole Ashes concept. England had no answer to the bowling of Fred Spofforth, who took fourteen wickets in the match to help Australia to a memorable seven-run victory.

Fourth Test, Adelaide, 1929

With the Ashes already won, Wally Hammond completed centuries in both innings for England, while nineteen-year-old Archie Jackson reached three figures on his debut for Australia – the youngest player to score an Ashes Test century. The outcome remained in the balance until Don Bradman was run out by Jack Hobbs and England crept home by twelve runs. Sadly, Jackson played just seven Tests before dying of tuberculosis at the age of twenty-three.

First Test, Sydney, 1894

Batting first, Australia compiled a mammoth 586, with Syd Gregory making a career-best 201 and sharing in a record ninth-wicket partnership of 154 in just 75 minutes with skipper Jack Blackham. England mustered 325 in reply and were forced to follow on. Their second innings of 437 set Australia a modest victory target of 177, and by the end of the fifth day Australia seemed comfortably placed, needing only another 64 to win. Several of the England players, including slow bowler Bobby Peel, relaxed accordingly, but captain Andrew Stoddart ordered Peel under a cold shower and on the sixth day he scythed through the Australian batting, taking 6 for 67 to give England a remarkable ten-run triumph.

Fourth Test, Melbourne, 1998–9

Following two heavy defeats, England partly redeemed themselves in the Fourth Test thanks to an unlikely bowling hero in Dean Headley. Trailing by 70 after the first innings, England went on to set Australia a mere 175 to win, but Headley – wicketless in the first innings – responded with 6 for 60 and, ably supported by the reliable Darren Gough, saw England to victory by twelve runs.

First Test, Sydney, 1887

Who could have predicted an England victory when they were skittled in their first innings for 45 (which remains their lowest Test score)? The side fared better second time around, eventually setting Australia a target of 111 to win, but the hosts remained firm favourites. Billy Barnes had other ideas, however, taking 6 for 28 from 46 overs, of which 29 were maidens, and England pulled off an astonishing thirteen-run success.

Third Test, Headingley, 1981

On the fourth day, following on, England had stumbled to 135–7, still 92 runs behind Australia. Ladbrokes clearly weren't being over-generous in offering odds of 500–1 on an England victory. But first

Ian Botham hit an awesome 149 not out, and then Bob Willis steamed in with patriotic passion to claim 8 for 43, and the shell-shocked Aussies were beaten by eighteen runs in the most incredible turnaround in Test match history.

Sixth Test, The Oval, 1997

With England 3–1 down in the series, the selectors recalled Phil Tufnell for the final Test, who responded by taking 11 wickets in the match. The previously dominant Australian batsmen were decimated by Tufnell and Andrew Caddick, guiding England to an improbable nineteen-run victory.

DATES WHEN FIRST-CLASS COUNTIES WERE FORMED

Sussex	1839
Nottinghamshire	1841
Surrey	1845
Kent	1859
Hampshire	1863
Yorkshire	1863
Lancashire	1864
Middlesex	1864
Worcestershire	1865
Derbyshire	1870
Gloucestershire	1871
Somerset	1875
Essex	1876
Northamptonshire	1878
Leicestershire	1879
Durham	1882
Warwickshire	1882
Glamorgan	1888

CRICKET AND THE CLOTH

THE ASSOCIATION between cricket and the church dates back to the very origins of the game, but few have combined the two disciplines with such zeal as former Leicestershire and England batsman Albert Knight. At the start of each innings Knight, who was a lay preacher, would sink to his knees at the crease and pray for help from above. When he played at Middlesex, this surely brought a new meaning to the Lord's Prayer. Despite occasional complaints from bowlers about his ritual, Knight's earthly reward was a career total of 18,142 runs and three England appearances.

Reverend E. F. 'Mick' Waddy was twelfth man for Australia against England at Sydney in the 1907–8 series, at the end of a season in which he topped the Australian first-class batting averages.

Reverend F. H. Gillingham made nineteen centuries for Essex in the early 1900s and in his capacity as honorary secretary of Worcestershire his brother, Reverend George Gillingham, once swam the River Severn, which had flooded the ground, to rescue the account books from the pavilion.

Jack Parsons played first-class cricket from 1910 to 1936 – principally for Warwickshire – and took holy orders in 1929, while Kent batsman Cecil Wilson later became Bishop of Bunbury, Australia.

But the most celebrated cricketing reverend was David Sheppard, who played 22 Tests for England between 1950 and 1963. He was ordained in 1955 and became Bishop of Woolwich in 1969. On one occasion, while the cricketing vicar was holding a baby during a christening ceremony, the infant's father remarked: 'I am a bit worried about you dropping my baby in the font given the sort of form you've been in this week.'

EDUCATING ARCHIE

As ENGLAND's Archie MacLaren hovered beneath an Australian batsman's skier, a member of the crowd shouted out: 'Miss it, Archie, and you can kiss me big sister!'

HIGHEST FOURTH-INNINGS TOTALS TO WIN A TEST

418–7	(set 418)	West Indies v Australia, St John's, 2002–3
406–4	(set 403)	India v West Indies, Port of Spain, 1975–6
404–3	(set 404)	Australia v England, Headingley, 1948
369–6	(set 369)	Australia v Pakistan, Hobart, 1999–2000
362–7	(set 359)	Australia v West Indies, Georgetown, 1977–8
348–5	(set 345)	West Indies v New Zealand, Auckland, 1968–9
344–1	(set 342)	West Indies v England, Lord's, 1984
342–8	(set 339)	Australia v India, Perth, 1977–8
340–5	(set 335)	South Africa v Australia, Durban, 2001–2
336–5	(set 336)	Australia v South Africa, Durban, 1949–50

NEVER TOO OLD

PLAYING for Wood Green in a home tie against United Willesden on 21 July 1872, fifty-five-year-old Charles Absolon had a hand in all twenty wickets. He bowled ten, two hit wicket, six were caught off his bowling, and he caught the remaining two as Wood Green won by an innings and 45 runs. The United Willesden scorecards read:

1ST INNINGS

Morley		b Absolon	1
Williams		b Absolon	0
Skipper	hit wicket	b Absolon	0
Parfitt	c Thomas	b Absolon	0
Bickwell	c Thomas	b Absolon	9
Bishop	c Absolon	b Wheeler	5
Digby		b Absolon	6
Lawrence	not out		0
Howard		b Absolon	0
Morris	hit wicket	b Absolon	2
Emerson	c Fluker	b Absolon	0
Extra			1
		Total	24

2ND INNINGS

Morley		b Absolon	6
Williams	c Absolon	b Fluker	7
Skipper		b Absolon	2
Parfitt		b Absolon	7
Bickwell		b Absolon	1
Bishop	c Chamberlain	b Absolon	0
Digby	c Ringrose	b Absolon	1
Lawrence		b Absolon	0
Howard		b Absolon	2
Morris	not out		1
Emerson	c Wheeler	b Absolon	0
Extras			4
		Total	31

Age could not wither the redoubtable Mr Absolon. He scored 1,029 runs and took 103 wickets in his seventy-second year, and at the age of seventy-eight he twice performed the hat-trick. As late as 1897, by which time he was eighty, he took 100 wickets in the season.

FATHER'S FUMBLE

DURING A TEST MATCH at Edgbaston in 2004, England's Andrew Flintoff hit a mighty six into the crowd, where a spectator made a gallant attempt to catch it. But very publicly, with the world's TV cameras on him, he dropped it. The hapless individual turned out to be Flintoff's father Colin.

SPOFFORTH'S SECRET

THE GREAT AUSTRALIAN CRICKETER Fred Spofforth was often asked how he came to be such an excellent fielder close to the wicket. He replied: 'When I was quite young I made a boy, when out for a walk, throw stones into a hedge, and as the sparrows flew out, I caught 'em!'

WORDS OF WISDOM

Cricket – a game which the English, not being a spiritual people, have invented in order to give themselves some conception of eternity.
LORD MANCROFT

There is a widely held and quite erroneous belief that cricket is just another game.
DUKE OF EDINBURGH

The very word 'cricket' has become a synonym for all that is true and honest. To say 'that is not cricket' implies something underhand, something not in keeping with the best ideals.
SIR PELHAM WARNER

It is surely the loveliest scene in England and the most disarming sound. From the ranks of the unseen dead for ever passing along our country lanes, the Englishman falls out for a moment to look over the gate of the cricket field and smile.
J. M. BARRIE

Few things are more deeply rooted in the collective imagination of the English than the village cricket match. It stirs a romantic illusion about the rustic way of life, it suggests a tranquil and unchanging order in an age of bewildering flux.
GEOFFREY MOORHOUSE

It's typical of English cricket. A tree gets in the way for two hundred years and, when it falls down, instead of cheering they plant a new one.
Former Australian fast bowler DAVID GILBERT
assessing Kent's new lime tree at Canterbury, 2005

It's a funny kind of month, October.
For the really keen cricket fan, it's when you realize
that your wife left you in May.
DENIS NORDEN

My wife had an uncle who could never walk down the nave
of an abbey without wondering whether it would take spin.
SIR ALEC DOUGLAS-HOME

It means I can drive a flock of sheep through the town centre,
drink for free in no less than sixty-four pubs and get a lift
home with the police when I become inebriated.
What more could you want?
ANDREW FLINTOFF,
on being granted the freedom of his hometown,
Preston, 2005

Not over till the fat laddie spins.
SUN *headline emphasizing* SHANE WARNE's *influence*
on the 2005 Ashes series

My diet is still pizzas, chips, toasted cheese sandwiches
and milkshakes. I have the occasional six-week burst
where I stick to fruit and cereal: it bloody kills me.
SHANE WARNE

Get a single down the other end
and watch someone else play him.
GEOFFREY BOYCOTT,
asked how best to deal with Glenn McGrath

The sight of Imran [Khan] tearing fearsomely down the hill
and the baying of the excited crowd made me realize for the
first time that adrenalin was sometimes brown.
SIMON HUGHES,
A Lot of Hard Yakka

It was a mixture of bad bowling, good shots and arse.
JASON GILLESPIE
sums up his 2005 Ashes series

His googly remains as hard to read as James Joyce.
PETER ROEBUCK *on Stuart MacGill*

As a Pom, he'd make a great Aussie.
JEFF THOMSON
expressing his admiration for Ian Botham

It's difficult to be more laid back than David Gower
without being actually comatose.
FRANCES EDMONDS

Denis Compton was the only player to call his partner
for a run and wish him good luck at the same time.
JOHN WARR

I'll tell you what pressure is.
Pressure is a Messerschmitt up your arse.
Playing cricket is not.
KEITH MILLER

It is rather suitable for umpires to dress like dentists,
since one of their tasks is to draw stumps.
JOHN ARLOTT

He was the first umpire to combine the distinct roles
of top-flight umpire and music-hall comedian.
MATTHEW ENGEL *on Dickie Bird*

The face of a choirboy, the demeanour of a civil servant
and the ruthlessness of a rat catcher.
GEOFFREY BOYCOTT
describing England teammate Derek Underwood

When you're an off-spinner there's not much point
glaring at a batsman. If I glared at Vivian Richards
he'd just hit me even further.
DAVID ACFIELD

A snick by Jack Hobbs is a sort of disturbance
of a cosmic orderliness.
SIR NEVILLE CARDUS

The hallmark of a great captain is the ability
to win the toss, at the right time.
RICHIE BENAUD

Being the manager of a touring team is rather like
being in charge of a cemetery – lots of people underneath
you, but no one listening.
WES HALL

There's nothing like the sound of flesh on leather
to get a cricket match going.
GEOFF LAWSON

A Test match is like a painting.
A one-day match is like a Rolf Harris painting.
IAN CHAPPELL

When you win the toss, bat. If you are in doubt,
think about it, then bat. If you have very big doubts,
consult a colleague – then bat.
W. G. GRACE

I don't like defensive shots, you can only get threes.
W. G. GRACE *(attrib.)*

I never wanted to make a hundred. Who wants to make
a hundred anyway? When I first went in, my immediate
objective was to hit the ball to each of the four corners
of the field. After that, I tried not to be repetitive.
LORD LEARIE CONSTANTINE

I don't think I've actually drunk a beer for fifteen years,
except a few Guinnesses in Dublin, where it's the law.
IAN BOTHAM, 2004

You can't smoke twenty a day and bowl fast.
PHIL TUFNELL *on why he became a spinner*

He could do the right things superbly, but when
he broke all the rules the ball still ended up at the fence.
BASIL EASTERBROOK *on Denis Compton*

You can't consider yourself a county cricketer
until you've eaten half a ton of lettuce.
SIR GARY SOBERS
on the staple diet of English county cricketers

ENGLAND RECORD TEST PARTNERSHIPS

1st	359	Len Hutton & Cyril Washbrook v South Africa, Johannesburg, 1948–9
2nd	382	Maurice Leyland & Len Hutton v Australia, Oval, 1938
3rd	370	Bill Edrich & Denis Compton v South Africa, Lord's, 1947
4th	411	Colin Cowdrey & Peter May v West Indies, Edgbaston, 1957
5th	254	Keith Fletcher & Tony Greig v India, Bombay, 1972–3
6th	281	Andrew Flintoff & Graham Thorpe v New Zealand, Christchurch, 2001–2
7th	197	Mike Smith & Jim Parks v West Indies, Port of Spain, 1959–60
8th	246	Les Ames & Gubby Allen v New Zealand, Lord's, 1931
9th	163*	Colin Cowdrey & Alan Smith v New Zealand, Wellington, 1962–3
10th	130	Reginald Foster & Wilfred Rhodes v Australia, Sydney, 1903–4

* not out

A Lesson
from the Australians

At the 1993 Oval Test against Australia, Graham Gooch fielded at short leg for the first time in years. After England had batted first, Gooch stifled Australia's reply by catching both Michael Slater and David Boon in that position. Afterwards, Gooch said to Boon, 'I'm glad that you blokes fielded first because I didn't know where to stand. But your footprints were out there, so I stood exactly where you did. I didn't even have to move – you hit it straight to me!'

Ways of Getting Out

Bowled
> Caught
>> Leg Before Wicket
>>> Stumped
>>>> Run Out
>>>>> Hit Wicket
>>>>>> Double Hit
>>>>>>> Timed Out
>>>>>>>> Obstructing the Field
>>>>>>>> Handled the Ball

Curiously, two England captains of recent years have been given out for handling the ball in Test matches. In June 1993, Graham Gooch had made 133 against Australia at Old Trafford when he played a ball from Merv Hughes down into his crease. As the ball bounced back towards his stumps, Gooch panicked and knocked it away with his hand. Law 33 states: 'Either batsman, on appeal, shall be out handled ball, if he wilfully touches the ball while in play with the hand not holding the bat, unless he does so with the consent of the opposite side.' So, when the Australians appealed, umpire Dickie Bird had no choice but to give Gooch out. Realizing later that he could have knocked the ball away with his foot without punishment, Gooch was no doubt kicking himself, particularly since his dismissal sparked an all-too-familiar England collapse. Eight years later, at Bangalore in December 2001, Michael Vaughan became the seventh batsman in Test cricket to be given out for handling the ball. He had made 64 when he missed a sweep at Indian spinner Sarandeep Singh. As the ball became tangled beneath him, Vaughan initially smothered it, then brushed it away from his crease. Although the ball wasn't heading for the stumps, the Indians were entitled to appeal – and did. Vaughan complained afterwards that the incident was 'against the spirit of the game'.

A RUSH FOR THE BOAT

WHEN THE WEST INDIES sent a team to England in 1900, among those selected as a batsman was L. S. Constantine, father of Learie Constantine. But on the day the boat left he was spotted wandering aimlessly downtown because he could not afford to go. A public subscription was opened on the spot, a fast launch was chartered and the tourists' boat was caught before it left the Gulf of Paria. Constantine scrambled on board, and at Lord's he became the first West Indian to make a century in England.

ODD DISMISSALS

- During the second Test against India at Kanpur in 1959, Australia's Neil Harvey caught Nari Contractor off a ball he never saw. He was fielding at short leg when the Indian pulled a delivery from Alan Davidson in his direction. Harvey turned his back and ducked, and the ball stuck between his thighs.

- Gloucestershire and England's Tom Goddard was run out twice in a match without receiving a single ball.

- In 1992, a batsman at Valparaiso Cricket Club, Chile, was given out after his lofted drive landed in the pocket of a white tennis cardigan being worn by one of the fielders.

- India's Mohinder Amarnath specialized in finding strange ways of getting out. He was out hit wicket three times in Tests, and in one-day internationals was given out for obstructing the field and also handling the ball.

- Batting for The Dominions against England at Lord's in August 1943, Learie Constantine was caught one-handed by Leslie Compton while the latter was leaning on the pavilion rails. The catch was ruled fair because Compton was standing inside the boundary when he caught the ball.

- In 1829 James Broadbridge literally threw his bat at a wide ball and was caught at point.

- Playing for Surrey against MCC at the Oval in 1870, James Southerton cut a ball hard into the ground from where it bounced into the hands of W. G. Grace at point. Although none of the fielders appealed, Southerton walked back to the pavilion and could not be persuaded to return. He was listed in the scorebook as having 'retired, thinking he was caught'.

- When Bishop Auckland's West Indian professional Ricky Waldren launched into a straight drive in a 1995 match, the ball ricocheted off the head of the umpire at the bowler's end, George Simpson, and was caught by a fielder on the boundary. While Waldren trudged back to the pavilion, Simpson was rushed to hospital to have ten stitches inserted in the wound.

- Fielding at short leg for Surrey at Kingston in 1946, Alf Gover took a catch from R. N. Exton (Combined Services) while in the act of pulling his sweater over his head. Unable to see a thing, Gover instinctively closed his legs on the ball. It was Jim Laker's first wicket in first-class cricket.

- In the 1970s, while batting at Kalgoorlie in Australia, Stan Dawson was hit by a quick delivery that ignited a box of matches in his pocket. As Dawson tried to put out the flames, an unsympathetic opposing fielder ran him out.

- In June 1896, England's Mr Stanley Jackson had scored 44 against Australia at Lord's when he deliberately gave his wicket away. After crowd encroachment had prevented Joe Darling catching him on the on side, the sporting Jackson immediately gave the fielder a second opportunity. The gesture did not backfire as England went on to win by six wickets.

- Former Warwickshire and England captain M. J. K. Smith was facing up to a ball against Hampshire at Edgbaston in 1962 when a sudden gust of wind whipped his cap from his head and on to his stumps. The unlucky batsman was given out 'hit wicket'.

- In 1930, Somerset's Cecil Case was given out 'hit wicket' in the match with Nottinghamshire at Taunton after falling on to the stumps while trying to get out of the way of a hostile delivery from Bill Voce. Case was so unnerved by the experience that he departed for the pavilion carrying a stump – rather than his bat – under his arm.

- Sussex batsman H. J. Heygate was timed out against Somerset at Taunton in 1919 because, crippled with rheumatism, he failed to reach the crease within the stipulated three minutes of the fall of the previous wicket.

An Actor's Tale

Harry Andrews remembers captaining a side against a women's team led by Peggy [Ashcroft]. The gentlemen batted left-handed and bowled underarm and the pre-arranged plan was that scores would finish level. The highly competitive Robert Shaw . . . would have none of this and swiped endless sixes. But, in the end, the Ian Botham of English acting was caught in the deep by Angela Baddeley. 'I didn't,' said Harry Andrews laconically, 'put Bob Shaw on to bowl.'

Peggy Ashcroft by Michael Billington

The Duckworth–Lewis Method – in Brief

The Duckworth–Lewis Method has been devised to satisfy those who believe that the game of cricket is just not complicated enough. Invented by statistician Frank Duckworth and lecturer

Tony Lewis (some would say, in a bad dream), the D/L Method has become the accepted way of determining the outcome of rain-interrupted one-day matches.

It operates on the principle that teams have two resources with which to make as many runs as possible – namely the number of overs they have still to receive and the number of wickets they have in hand. If an innings is interrupted and has to be shortened, the balance of resources is upset, as a result of which a revised target is necessary to compensate the team that has suffered the greater loss. The target adjustment is based on the relative run-scoring resources available to the two teams after the resources lost by each have been taken into account. Where stoppages cause the team batting second to have fewer resources available, their target will be revised downwards. Conversely if, as is often the case when the team batting first have their innings interrupted, the stoppages result in the team batting second having more resources available, their target is revised upwards. The D/L table also takes into account when the interruption occurs, since a loss of overs near the end of an innings, particularly when there are plenty of wickets in hand, is usually a far greater loss of resource than the same loss of overs at the start of an innings.

Extract from the table of resource percentages remaining:

overs left	0 wkts lost	2 wkts lost	5 wkts lost	9 wkts lost
50	100.0	83.8	49.5	7.6
40	90.3	77.6	48.3	7.6
30	77.1	68.2	45.7	7.6
20	58.9	54.0	40.0	7.6
10	34.1	32.5	27.5	7.5

Since 50-over matches are the most common, the resources listed in the D/L table are expressed as percentages of those available at the start of a 50-over innings. Thus when there are 50 overs still to be bowled and no wickets have fallen, the resource percentage available is 100 per cent. However a 40-over innings starts with a resource percentage of 90.3, a 30-over innings with 77.1 per cent, and

so on. In the event of an interruption, the number of wickets lost must also be taken into consideration. To calculate the resources lost from an innings, the position at the resumption of play is subtracted from that at the point of interruption. So if Team 1 batted first and made 230 from 50 overs, and Team 2 in reply reached 115–2 after 30 overs when rain halted play for 10 overs, the table would be used to work out the resources lost. Two wickets down with 20 overs remaining is 54.0 per cent and when play resumed 10 overs later (i.e. with 10 overs remaining), the figure is reduced to 32.5 per cent. Therefore, the total resources lost are 54.0 minus 32.5, which equals 21.5 per cent. This figure is then deducted from that at the start of the innings (100 per cent) to leave Team 2 with only 78.5 per cent of available resources, compared with Team 1's 100 per cent. So Team 2's revised target becomes 78.5 per cent of 230, which, rounded up to the nearest whole number, is 181.

This is the essence of the Duckworth–Lewis Method. There are variations for different scenarios, but life's too short for some things . . .

A Costly Miscalculation

ONE PERSON who fell spectacularly foul of the Duckworth–Lewis Method was South Africa's Shaun Pollock. Telling Mark Boucher he had only to block the final ball against Sri Lanka in the group stages of the 2003 World Cup, Pollock believed South Africa were through to the Super Six stage. But he miscalculated the Duckworth–Lewis system, and the resulting tie instead sent his country out of the competition. Pollock's captaincy came to an abrupt end.

Death and Cricket

- Cricket's first fatality occurred on 28 August 1624. Jasper Vinall and Edward Tye, from West Hoathly in Sussex, were playing 'crickett' with various others on Horsted Green in the neighbouring village of Horsted Keynes. After lofting the ball up into the air with his bat, Tye tried to hit again as it dropped, unaware that Vinall was running up behind him in an attempt to catch the ball. The bat made contact with Vinall's head, causing a wound from which he died on 10 September. The inquest ruled that he had been killed by misadventure and through his own carelessness.

- On 7 June 1731, Mr Legat, a cooper and dealer in brandy and rum, was passing what became the Honourable Artillery Company's ground in London when he was struck on the nose by a cricket ball, which had been hit over the wall. The blow caused profuse bleeding from which he died a month later.

- Playing for Nottinghamshire against the MCC at Lord's in June 1870, George Summers died after being hit on the cheekbone by a ball from John Platts, a Derbyshire fast bowler making his first-class debut. Above Summers' grave at Nottingham, the MCC erected a memorial tablet 'testifying their sense of his qualities as a cricketer and regret at the untimely accident on Lord's ground'.

- Seventeen-year-old Hamilton Plumptre Lighton, son of Reverend Sir Christopher Lighton, was killed playing cricket for Repton Hall School in 1872. He was bowling to fellow pupil Richard Sale, whose fiercely hit return reared up and struck the bowler on the side of the head just above the right ear. Lighton died from his injuries that night.

- The *Wisden* entry for the 1934 County Championship match between Essex and Worcestershire read: 'On Whit Monday morning Nichol, the Worcestershire batsman, was found dead in bed – a sad event that marred the enjoyment of the match, but did not prevent Worcestershire gaining first-innings lead.'

- The wartime game between Surrey Home Guard and Sussex Home Guard at Lord's on 23 July 1942 was

abandoned after Andy Ducat, the Surrey and England cricketer and international footballer, collapsed and died, bat in hand, at the wicket. Ducat had made 29 when he played a ball to mid-on. The ball was returned to bowler Eaton, who was about to send down the next delivery when Ducat suddenly slumped forward, dead. The fifty-six-year-old had suffered a heart attack.

- Twenty-year-old Indian umpire Uday Vasant Pimple was killed by an irate wicketkeeper after rejecting his appeal in a match at Nagpur in 1987. The wicketkeeper disputed the umpire's decision and then smashed him over the head with a stump.

- After being injured in the first innings of the 1958–9 Qaid-I-Azam Trophy final in Karachi, Abdul Aziz was listed in the scorebook as: 'Abdul Aziz retired hurt . . . o.' The injury proved fatal, however, and so the scorer, leaving no room for misinterpretation, recorded for the second innings: 'Abdul Aziz did not bat, dead . . . o.'

NOTABLE CRICKET SUICIDES

WILLIAM SCOTTON (Nottinghamshire and England) drowned himself in Thames, December 1888

ARTHUR SHREWSBURY* (Nottinghamshire and England) shot himself, May 1903

ALBERT TROTT (Middlesex and Australia) shot himself, July 1914

ANDREW STODDART* (Middlesex and England) shot himself, April 1915

BILL ZULCH (Transvaal and South Africa) slit his own throat, May 1924

WILLIAM BRUCE* (Victoria and Australia) drowned himself in the sea, August 1925

AUBREY FAULKNER (South Africa) carbon monoxide poisoning, September 1930

JACK CUFFE (Worcestershire and Australia) drowned himself, May 1931

BERT RELF (Sussex and England) shot himself, March 1937

GEORGE SHEPSTONE (South Africa) shot himself, July 1940

TOMMY COOK (Sussex and England) overdose of tablets, January 1950

JACK IVERSON (Victoria and Australia) shot himself, October 1973

SID BARNES (NSW and Australia) overdose of barbiturates, December 1973

HAROLD GIMBLETT (Somerset and England) overdose, March 1978

JIMMY BURKE (NSW and Australia) shot himself, February 1979

NOEL HARFORD (Auckland and New Zealand), car exhaust fumes, March 1981

COTAR RAMASWAMI (India) disappeared after leaving suicide notes, October 1985

STUART LEARY (Kent) threw himself off Table Mountain, South Africa, August 1988

SUNIL JAYASINGHE (Sri Lanka) poisoned himself, April 1995

DAVID BAIRSTOW (Yorkshire and England) hanged himself, January 1998

*As Stoddart and Shrewsbury walked out to open the batting for England on 17 July 1893, they passed Australia's Bruce in the field – a macabre gathering of three future suicides.

[69]

Wisden
OBITUARY FROM 1965

CAT, PETER, whose ninth life ended on November 5, 1964, was a well-known cricket-watcher at Lord's, where he spent twelve of his fourteen years. He preferred a close-up view of proceedings and his sleek, black form could often be seen prowling on the field of play when the crowds were biggest. He frequently appeared on the television screen. Mr S. C. Griffith, Secretary of MCC, said of him, 'He was a cat of great character and loved publicity.'

A FARCICAL ENCOUNTER

BEFORE THE DECLARATION RULE was introduced in 1889, teams would blatantly sacrifice wickets in the hope of forcing a result. Occasionally this produced a farcical situation, as when Surrey met Sussex at the Oval in August 1887. Leading by 45 on first innings, Sussex were dismayed as Surrey piled up the runs on the final day and, on a damp pitch, feared defeat when it was their turn to bat. So they tried to prolong the Surrey innings, Bean deliberately bowling eight no-balls in one over to waste time. For their part, the last few Surrey batsmen had been told to get out quickly but their number ten, Bowley, kept charging down the pitch so ridiculously that the Sussex wicketkeeper Dudney refused to stump him. Eventually the frustrated Bowley deliberately trod on his wicket to bring the Surrey innings to a close at 4.45 p.m. This left Sussex needing to survive for 1 hour 25 minutes in deteriorating light, which they managed to do by struggling through to 61–7 at the close to save the match.

THE PERFECT OVER

The first delivery was short of a length and gloved me, bouncing well in front of the slips; the second was short, and I played and missed as it bounced; the third nipped back and hit me on the inside of the left thigh; the fourth bounced and I played it down in front of gully; the fifth was an action replay of the fourth; the sixth plucked my off stump crazily out of the ground.

GEOFF BOYCOTT *describing a memorable opening over from Michael Holding in the third Test on England's 1981 tour of the West Indies*

A DAMP WICKET

ON 1 AUGUST 1983, Oval groundsman Harry Brind spotted a man urinating on the wicket. The police were called and Robert Shedan, a thirty-two-year-old engineer, was charged with causing criminal damage to the Oval wicket. He was fined £10 and ordered to pay £10 compensation to Surrey County Cricket Club, who had to relay the damaged area of the pitch.

WICKETKEEPERS
WITH MOST TEST DISMISSALS

	Matches	Caught	Stumped	Total
IAN HEALY (Australia)	119	366	29	395
ROD MARSH (Australia)	96	343	12	355
ADAM GILCHRIST (Australia)	79	301	32	333
MARK BOUCHER (South Africa)	85	311	14	325
ALEC STEWART (England)	133	263	14	277
JEFF DUJON (West Indies)	81	267	5	272
ALAN KNOTT (England)	95	250	19	269
WASIM BARI (Pakistan)	81	201	27	228
RIDLEY JACOBS (West Indies)	65	207	12	219
GODFREY EVANS (England)	91	173	46	219

SCHOOLBOY CRICKET

IN HIS 1862 BOOK *School Days of Eminent Men*, John Timbs wrote that cricket was played at Winchester School around 1655. By 1710, Thomas Blomer, a fellow of Trinity College, Cambridge, was complaining of students hurrying their meals so that they could go and play football or cricket. The game soon established itself in the public schools and universities of England, its importance illustrated by a letter written by the Earl of Chesterfield to his son at Westminster in 1742: '. . . for if you have a right ambition you will desire to excel all boys of your age at cricket, or trap-ball, as well as in learning.' The first known inter-school match was between Charterhouse and Westminster at the old Lord's ground in Dorset Square on 5 August 1794. The match was played for 500 guineas, Westminster winning handsomely by an innings and 105 runs. The pastime was not approved of in all quarters, however – not least the drunken horse-play that frequently accompanied it at public school level – and when the headmaster of Eton discovered that his boys had arranged a secret cricket match with Westminster on Hounslow Heath in 1807, he flogged the entire team.

PROMISING PUPILS

A WORLD RECORD PARTNERSHIP of 664 runs unbroken for the third wicket was compiled by two schoolboys during the Harris Shield tournament for Bombay schools in February 1988. Vinod Kambli, a sixteen-year-old left-hander, and fourteen-year-old Sachin Tendulkar were playing for Sharadashram Vidyamandir (English) against St Xavier's High School. Kambli hit three sixes and 49 fours in his innings of 349 not out, and Tendulkar hit one six and 48 fours in compiling an undefeated 326. Kambli followed up by taking 6 for 37 with off-breaks to dismiss St Xavier's for 145 and give his school a 603-run victory.

Just as Tendulkar showed youthful signs of future greatness, it was reported that Andrew Flintoff, a pupil at Ribbleton Hall High School, Preston, once hit 234 not out in only 20 overs (including 20 sixes and 20 fours) for St Anne's under-15s against Fulwood and Broughton.

*A cricketer Lord's-bound from Yeovil
Turned up by mistake at the Eovil;
So he said, 'Never worry,'
And batted for Surrey
Though this met with some disappreovil.*

DOROTHY SPRING

SIX FAMOUS FEUDS

Roy Gilchrist and Swaranjit Singh

HEARING that Singh had apparently been bad-mouthing him, West Indian Gilchrist bowled him a series of hostile beamers and bouncers in a match prior to the 1958–9 Test series in India. Gilchrist refused to apologize, and when his captain Gerry Alexander, who had been at Cambridge with Singh, ordered him to stop bowling beamers, Gilchrist ignored him. While the rest of the team moved on to Pakistan at the end of the tour, Gilchrist was sent home. The episode marked the end of his Test career.

Dennis Lillee and Sunil Gavaskar

CONTROVERSIALLY given out lbw to Lillee in the 1980–1 series, the Indian captain exchanged angry words with the bowler before trudging back towards the pavilion. On the way, he claimed Lillee abused him, at which point Gavaskar asked non-striker Chetan Chauhan to walk off the field, thereby forfeiting the match. Fortunately, Gavaskar calmed down and India went on to claim a historic triumph.

Dennis Lillee and Javed Miandad

LILLEE was involved in another fracas at Perth on Pakistan's 1981–2 tour when he kicked Javed Miandad's pads as the batsman went by for a single. The volatile Mianded reacted by trying to attack Lillee with his bat, necessitating the intervention of umpire Tony Crafter. Henry Blofeld wrote in *The Cricketer:* 'I very much doubt if there has ever been a more unpleasant incident in a Test match than that at Perth when Lillee first deliberately blocked the Pakistan captain as he was completing a single and then launched a kick at him when he had made his crease. Over the years Lillee has been involved in probably more unpleasant incidents than any other Test cricketer. He has seemed almost to make a habit of trying to bait and upset his opponents in the most petulant manner.'

Geoff Lawson and Desmond Haynes

SICK of being battered by the West Indian pacemen, Australia retaliated by trying to intimidate opponents verbally. Fast bowler Lawson provoked Haynes to such an extent at Brisbane on the 1984–5 tour that Haynes replied with a two-fingered gesture, an incident for which Lawson was fined AUS$2,000.

Merv Hughes and Mike Atherton

MASTER sledger Hughes saw the young, fresh-faced Atherton as perfect victim material when their two countries clashed in 1989. Atherton later wrote: 'He snarled at me constantly through his ludicrous moustache. He was all bristle and bullshit and I couldn't make out what he was saying, except that every sledge ended with "arsewipe".' Atherton sensibly decided that the best policy was simply to smile back and save his energy.

Shane Warne and Daryll Cullinan

THE South African had tried to dish out some fat-boy jibes, but was soon forced to eat humble pie as he became Warne's personal bunny. After Cullinan admitted in a 1997 interview that he had sought psychiatric help, Warne vowed to send him straight back to the leather couch. Cullinan was out for a duck and missed the rest of the series.

THE PARIS OLYMPICS

CRICKET MADE its solitary appearance in the Olympic Games in Paris in 1900. The competition consisted of just one match, played between Britain (represented by the Devon and Somerset Wanderers CC) and France, made up of staff from the British Embassy in Paris. Not surprisingly, perhaps, Britain won by 158 runs, although none of the players were aware of the game's Olympic status until some months later.

BROADCASTING CRICKET

The first cricket match to be broadcast in this country will be that between Essex and New Zealand at Leyton on 14 May. Recognizing that to attempt anything like a full description of the play, as in a football match, would be boring in the extreme, the BBC intend to deal with the event piecemeal.

From 2.10 until 2.20 p.m. the commentator, the Reverend F. H. Gillingham, will give the names of the teams, describe the condition of the ground, and so on. After that there will be four five-minute descriptions of the actual play – from 3 p.m. to 3.05 p.m., 4 p.m. to 4.05 p.m., 5 p.m. to 5.05 p.m. and 6 p.m. to 6.05 p.m.

At 6.45 p.m. there will be a general summary of the play. In addition listeners may be switched over to the ground at any period when play is specially interesting. The microphone will not be placed in a hut, but will be fixed at the left-hand corner of the balcony outside the secretary's office in the pavilion. In this way a background of subdued noises will be obtained, though the noises will not be sufficient to interfere with the broadcast.

Manchester Guardian, 1927

IN FACT the BBC's first tentative dip into the murky waters of cricket broadcasting came five years after Australia had conducted an experiment in commentary. Reporting from Sydney Cricket Ground on a 1922 testimonial match for Charles Bannerman, Len Watt was handed a microphone and simply told to carry on talking. In December 1924, the experiment was extended to Test cricket when Hyam Marks and Clem Hill gave 'commentary and scores' on the Ashes series on Sydney's local 2BL radio station, no doubt discussing that this was the first occasion that eight-ball overs had been bowled in Test cricket. The term 'ball-by-ball' was first used in 1925, when Watt commentated on the Australia v The Rest Test trial, using a microphone suspended from the boundary fence at Sydney.

Not content with covering home internationals, the ambitious Australians expanded their network to give ball-by-ball commentary on the Ashes series in England, even though, in the early days at least, their commentators never actually ventured further than the Sydney studios. The action was relayed via cables sent from England at the end of each over, giving brief details of each ball. The information in the cable was then hastily decoded and described by the commentators as if they were witnessing the play. Alan McGilvray, one of the pioneers at the microphone, described this primitive art: 'A cable which read "HAMMOND SWEPT BARNES FOUR" might end up "Hammond sweeps him. He's really got on to that one and Barnes is tearing around the boundary to cut it off, but I don't think he'll get it, and he doesn't, and the ball just beats him over the boundary rope for four."' The score was kept on a big board in the studio, complete with bowling figures, and the ingenious team even produced their own sound effects. Crowd reactions were pre-recorded, but the commentators themselves provided the sound of bat on ball by hitting a piece of wood with a pencil, the force of the pencil strike imitating the power of the stroke. Inevitably, the odd mistake occurred. Once, on reading a cable that said 'MC' was out, McGilvray gambled on the assumption that the initials referred to Stan McCabe, and delivered a vivid description of his dismissal to the listeners, only to discover from the next cable that the 'MC' in question was teammate Ernie McCormick.

The BBC's *Test Match Special* made its debut on the Third Programme in 1957, covering the series between England and the West Indies, the *Radio Times* slogan being 'Don't miss a ball, we broadcast them all.' The commentary team comprised Rex Alston, John Arlott, Ken Ablack, Gerry Gomez and Bill Bowes, with E. W. (Jim) Swanton providing a summary of the day's play. From 1970, when he was dropped by BBC Television, chocolate-cake-loving Brian Johnston was to become the arch prankster of the *Test Match Special* team. On one occasion he set up Alan McGilvray beautifully. 'Have a piece of this delightful chocolate cake, McGillers,' Johnston said on air in his famously informal way. Then, as McGilvray was happily negotiating a large mouthful, Johnston announced, 'Now, for a description of that last dismissal, I hand you over to Alan . . .' Jonathan Agnew was once asked to do a ten-minute interview for BBC TV's *Grandstand* with Fred Trueman and Jack Bannister about England's dearth of fast bowlers. Bannister was distinctly uncooperative, while Trueman started rambling on about damp courses and salmon fishing. Agnew was perspiring freely as the head of BBC TV cricket yelled in his earpiece that it was the worst interview he had ever seen. It was only afterwards that Agnew learned that the whole episode had been a practical joke lovingly arranged by Johnners.

REMARKABLE ACHIEVEMENTS

- PLAYING AGAINST WILLINGHAM, Cambridgeshire, in July 1874, Godmanchester fast bowler Charles Brawn took six wickets in six balls. Willingham were 20–0 when Brawn trapped Elwood leg before, and with his next two deliveries he bowled Askew and Thoddy. That marked the end of the over, but with the first three balls of his next over he clean-bowled Few, Frohock and Gleaves.

- Batting for Clarke's against North Town in a junior house match at Clifton College in June 1899, A. E. Collins made 628 not out in a total of 836. He batted for 6 hours 50 minutes. Clarke's won by an innings and 688 runs.

- In the 1912 Varsity match at Lord's, Oxford University's Gerald Crutchley had made 99 not out when he ran out of partners. On returning to the pavilion he was found to be suffering from a severe case of measles and played no further part in the game. Cambridge won by three wickets.

- In the summer of 1947 Denis Compton made 18 centuries in 50 innings, scoring 3,816 runs at an average of 90.85. For good measure he bowled 635.4 overs, taking 73 wickets, and also held 31 catches.

- Playing for Hampshire against Warwickshire at Southampton in 1926, George Brown split the blade of his bat in two. That didn't stop him from playing, however, and after handing one half to the umpire he continued to bat on with the other half.

- When Yorkshire entertained Leicestershire at Huddersfield in 1919, the Yorkshire twelfth man, Bill Williams, acted as a substitute for Leicestershire and caught out four of his own team.

- India's R. G. Nadkarni returned bowling figures of 31–27–5–0 against England at Madras in 1964. The English batsmen said he was 'unhittable'.

- In making 164 for Australia against Middlesex at Lord's in 1926, Tommy Andrews was caught three times off no-balls.

- When Kevin Pietersen reached 500 runs in just nine one-day internationals, he equalled the record set by another England batsman, Dennis Amiss.

- F. C. Cobden of Cambridge University performed a hat-trick to win the 1870 Varsity match at a time when Oxford needed just two runs for victory.

- England's Graham Gooch is the only batsman to score more than 2,000 Test runs on a single ground. He made 2,015 runs in 21 Tests at Lord's, including six centuries.

- Despite having only one leg, Norman Waterworth, captain of Gisburn CC, Lancashire, took over 1,000 wickets and made 3,600 runs in 22 seasons.

DEGREES BELOW ZERO

Duck: out for nought, the zero resembling a duck's egg.

Pair: dismissed for a duck in both innings, so called because of the supposed resemblance of the two noughts in a scorebook to a pair of spectacles.

Golden duck: out first ball.

King pair: out first ball in both innings.

Emperor pair: a 'pair' recorded by an opening batsman who is dismissed without scoring to the first ball of both innings.

MOST TEST WICKETS
TAKEN BOWLED

Muttiah Muralitharan (Sri Lanka)	137
Shane Warne (Australia)	108
Fred Trueman (England)	103
Brian Statham (England)	102
Waqar Younis (Pakistan)	102
Wasim Akram (Pakistan)	102
Ray Lindwall (Australia)	98
Imran Khan (Pakistan)	96
Richard Hadlee (New Zealand)	92
Courtney Walsh (West Indies)	91
Kapil Dev (India)	89
Lance Gibbs (West Indies)	87
Curtly Ambrose (West Indies)	83
Michael Holding (West Indies)	81
Derek Underwood (England)	79
Malcolm Marshall (West Indies)	73
Glenn McGrath (Australia)	71
Alec Bedser (England)	70
Anil Kumble (India)	70
Joel Garner (West Indies)	69
Graham McKenzie (Australia)	69

THE LEISURELY APPROACH

PAKISTAN CAPTAIN Inzamam-ul-Haq is renowned for his aversion to physical exercise. In 2000, when Pakistan were practising before a Test, Inzy stayed in the dressing-room while the rest of the team went out for their warm-up and fielding drill. As they moved on to the nets, Inzy ventured outside, walking slowly to a large wicker chair that had been placed, caringly, for him alongside the nets. When it was his turn to bat, he hauled himself slowly from his chair, dealt with each delivery with the minimum of effort, then returned to the dressing-room. Next day he scored a century.

CRICKET IN CORFU

WHEN CORFU fell under the British flag in the early nineteenth century, naturally one of the first requirements was for the islanders to learn to play cricket. On 23 April 1823, Corfu staged a match between the officers of the British Navy and the Garrison, and within twelve years the locals had mastered the game to the extent that two Corfiot teams had been formed to challenge the British. *The Times* of 14 December 1859 reported: 'Corfu has this year been visited by an extraordinary number of fashionable tourists – politician, artistic and sporting. The latter are the most numerous.'

Although the British left in 1864 their cricketing legacy lived on, principally through the Gymnastikos and Ergatikos clubs, who regularly played against visiting British sailors. In 1904 the Mediterranean fleet of some forty ships attended the island's cricket festival. With new air routes opening up in the 1960s, Corfu became a popular destination for British cricket clubs on tour and in 1962 the island hosted an International XI featuring such names as Wes Hall, Rohan Kanhai, Bill Alley and Basil d'Oliveira.

The annual cricket festival is still a key event in the Corfu calendar. The pitch in Corfu Town consists of matting on concrete. Three sides of the playing area are bordered by a tarmac car park, a local rule stating that a four is scored whenever a ball goes under a car. Games usually finish in moonlight.

Some Corfiot cricketing terms:

Afini palla ('to leave the bat'): a declaration

Apo podi ('from the foot'): out lbw

Apo psila ('from high'): out caught

Apo xyla ('from the wood'): out bowled

How 'dat: this is used both in appealing (like 'howzat') and also to state that the appeal against the batsman has been upheld (like 'out')

Pintz: a Yorker

Tapetto ('mat' or 'carpet'): the pitch, because games in Corfu are generally played on matting.

From *Creatures of Circumstances* by Horace Hutchinson (1891)

HORACE HUTCHINSON, the author of the first cricket novel, *Peter Steele, The Cricketer,* here describes an annual encounter between Little Pipkin and White-Cross. Following heavy defeats the previous two years, Little Pipkin's Colonel Burscough had suggested that the match should, as tradition dictated, be played solely between villagers, but Lord Morningham, for White-Cross, insisted on continuing his recent practice of inviting players from outside. Therefore, the Colonel decided to play him at his own game.

On the day of the great match Lord Morningham drove over in his dog-cart with two of his friends, betimes, and another friend, and the rest of the eleven of White-Cross, in a drag, were not long behind him. When they came out of the dressing-tent the eleven of White-Cross presented a splendour that charmed the eye with the colours of the I. Zingari, Free Foresters and MCC adorning the persons of the three imported crick-eters; while the appearance of the eleven of Little Pipkin was of pure, unrelieved rusticity. But some of the men of White-Cross began to ask one another who was that rustic with the long legs and the hat pulled over his eyes; and who that one with the stout legs? There was also a third who was a stranger to them, but he escaped general notice because he was of little stature. They asked the men of Little Pipkin who these men were, and some said, quite truly, that they did not know, and others that the strangers had but lately come to the village; and this again was true, for they had come to it but the night before.

White-Cross won the toss, and Lord Morningham sat in the pavilion and watched the first of his friends, who was a mighty swiper, go in, and settled himself to see him swipe. The long-legged stranger rustic began to bowl. At the first ball Lord Morningham whistled after a manner he had when in the pavilion at Lord's; for he affected cricket, as being a popular game, and because he had been the coolest slow bowler for an Eton boy that had ever trundled out a Harrow eleven. But he whistled because the ball went so fearfully near the wicket. To the second ball the batsman played forward carefully, and met it. But the third pitched a trifle shorter, and the batsman, playing forward as before, returned it to the hands of the bowler, where it remained.

The most terrible catastrophes are those that happen most suddenly, and in quick succession the wickets fell of the other two whose names were great at Lord's, and they were together in the pavilion explaining to each other the causes of their several downfalls, which they agreed in attributing to luck, and expressed every confidence that, given another trial, they could go on playing that sort of bowling all day long. For the other bowler was the stranger rustic who had escaped notice by his shortness of stature.

Disheartened by the defeat of their best and brightest, the eleven of White-Cross were all out for twenty-seven, and byes had contributed most of these. Then it was the turn of Little Pipkin to go in, and the short stranger rustic and the stout-legged stranger rustic went to the wickets. And despite all the efforts of the friends of Lord Morningham, whose names were so great at Lord's, they were at the wickets still when the luncheon bell rang; and most of this time had been spent by the eleven of White-Cross, assisted by the entire village of Little Pipkin, in hunting for the ball in the hedge of the vicarage glebe, into which these stranger rustics repeatedly hit it. And the telegraph read 137, and that only, for of wickets fallen there was no tale to tell. At the beginning of luncheon the strangers were conspicuous by their absence, but after a short time they came in, no longer in their rustic garb, but in the unclouded majesty of white flannel. And Lord Morningham and his friends at once recognized them, and gave a shout, for the long rustic was a very famous bowler of the Surrey eleven, and the stout-legged rustic was the best batsman on a mud-wicket in all England (the champion not excepted), and the rustic of short stature was the most brilliant fieldsman of the eleven of Lancashire, and good with bat and ball alike.

FIELDING POSITIONS: THEIR ORIGINS

THE USE OF THE WORDS 'on' and 'off' stems from the 'off side' and 'near side' of a horse or carriage, the off side being the opposite side to which a driver walks or the rider mounts. Some early cricket writers referred to the near side when describing the on or leg side but the term gradually faded from use.

SLIPS: The origin of the slips is hinted at in an early description of the long stop, who 'is required to cover many slips from the bat'. Early cricket writers identified two slip positions in the game – short-slip, which was equivalent to the present-day first or second slip, and long-slip, similar to a modern short third man or fly-slip.

POINT: This is an abbreviation of 'point of the bat', a position whereby the fielder stood close to the end of the batsman's bat. Indeed the position was originally called 'bat's end'.

GULLY: The name apparently derives from the general meaning of gully, suggesting a narrow channel between point and the slips.

COVER: The fielder in this position used to be known as the 'man who covers the point and middle wicket'.

MID-ON and **MID-OFF:** These terms are a contraction of the early-nineteenth-century positions 'middle wicket off' and 'middle wicket on'.

SILLY: On account of its close proximity to the batsman, a 'silly' position (e.g. silly mid-off, silly point) is generally thought to take its name from the folly of fielding there. However, the *Oxford English Dictionary* also lists a now obsolete – but equally apt – use of silly to mean 'defenceless'.

THIRD MAN: This position became popular with the spread of overarm bowling and the development of bowling at or just outside the off stump. To supplement the established close offside fielding positions of point and short-slip, another fielder was placed behind them. He was thus the third man up.

LONG STOP: Obsolete from the game at Test level for over a hundred years, the position of long stop was once an important back-up to the wicketkeeper. Before wicketkeeping evolved into a specialist art, bowlers would often take turns to stand behind the stumps, as a result of which the standard of wicketkeeping was not very high. But as playing surfaces improved and the skill of wicketkeepers developed, the long stop became redundant.

The Joys of the Cricket Field

Few men in their whole lives are so fortunate as to feel a moment of keener joy than a successful boy-cricketer in such an hour of triumph; it is without alloy; the only Nemesis he need fear is 'a pair of spectacles' in his next match, and to avert that he need not now crawl on his knees up the pavilion steps. Nor will the severest philosophy blame his exultation. He has done best what all his schoolfellows are eager to do well, and for doing which well even his masters, who have not forgotten that they too have been boys and cricketers, are proud of, and even grateful to him. The whole scene is English; the public schools are English; the game is English; the feelings it excites and the demonstrations of them which it prompts are English; and in the energy with which victory is sought, in the elation of those who achieve it, in the patient good humour of the defeated party, and in the sympathy of the spectators with both, we see a fair sample of the manly, good-tempered, honest character which pervades the whole of our nation, and is the parent of success in more important fields of action.

The Shilling Magazine, August 1865

An Idea for the Scorers

BRIAN JOHNSTON suggested on *Test Match Special* that if batsman and wicketkeeper missed a ball from that fine Indian spinner Bishen Bedi, any runs should be recorded as 'Bedi byes'.

The Single-Pad Riddle

At a cricket match the other day, a batsman went in with only one pad on. Noticing it adorned the right leg, the fielders assumed he was a left-hander and altered their positions accordingly. But he turned out to be right-handed after all, so the wicketkeeper pointed out to him that he had the pad on the wrong leg. 'Nothing of the sort,' was the reply. 'You see, I thought I was going in at the other end.'

Cologne Post, August 1922

Umpires Who Have Officiated in Most Tests

Steve Bucknor (West Indies)	108
David Shepherd (England)	92
Srinivas Venkataraghavan (India)	73
Rudi Koertzen (South Africa)	69
Darrell Hair (Australia)	68
Dickie Bird (England)	66
Daryl Harper (Australia)	54
Frank Chester (England)	48
David Orchard (South Africa)	44
Charlie Elliott (England)	42

CLIMATE CHANGE

THAT MOST STYLISH of batsmen, the Indian prince Kumar Shri Ranjitsinhji, may have mastered English bowlers, but he struggled to cope with the English climate. The summer of 1912 was generally cold and wet, and, with the wind whipping off the North Sea, the Scarborough Festival that year was definitely a place for the hardy. Having just returned from tropical India, Ranji took the precaution of buying an extra layer of clothing for fielding duties. First he wore an extra vest, then a woollen waistcoat, which made him seem as though he was rapidly putting on weight as the day progressed. *The Times* observed: 'Had the cold lasted, he certainly would not have been able to pass out of the dressing-room door.'

WOMEN'S CRICKET

WOMEN'S CRICKET has always been more than just an appendage to the men's game. After all, the first Women's World Cup was staged in 1973 – two years before the men's version. Indeed, the first report of a women's cricket match appeared in the *Reading Mercury* as early as 26 July 1745. 'The greatest cricket match that was ever played in the South part of England was on Friday, the 26th of last month, on Gosden Common, near Guildford, in Surrey, between eleven maids of Bramley and eleven maids of Hamble-ton, dressed all in white. The Bramley maids had blue ribbons and the

Hambleton maids red ribbons on their heads. The Bramley girls got 119 notches and the Hambleton girls 127. There was of bothe sexes the greatest number that ever was seen on such an occasion. The girls bowled, batted, ran and catches as well as most men could do in that game.'

The first women's cricket club, the White Heather Club, was formed in 1887 at Nun Appleton in Yorkshire. It started out with just eight members, but within three years that figure had increased to fifty, among the number being Lucy Ridsdale, later Mrs Stanley Baldwin. The year 1890 also saw the appearance of two teams of professional women cricketers whose talents were advertised in several periodicals. The advertisement ran: 'With the object of providing the suitability of the National Game as a pastime for the fair sex in preference to Lawn Tennis and other less scientific games, the English Cricket and Athletic Association Ltd have organized two complete elevens of female players under the title of THE ORIGINAL ENGLISH LADY CRICKETERS.' Known as the Red XI and the Blue XI, the girls were forbidden to use their real names and were chaperoned by a matron wherever they went. Coached by male professionals, they were paid £1 15s a week, plus expenses of up to 1s a day. A crowd of 15,000 turned up to watch the Original English Lady Cricketers play their first match at Liverpool, and they went on to embark on a successful nationwide tour. By the summer of 1891, however, the novelty had worn off and the OELC was disbanded.

The Women's Cricket Association was founded in 1926 and the first overseas tour was made to Australia and New Zealand in 1934–5, featuring the inaugural women's Test match between Australia and England at Brisbane in December 1934. Batting first, Australia slumped to 13–5 and were finally dismissed for 47, Myrtle Maclagan taking 7 for 10. She then opened the batting for England and top-scored with 72 in a total of 154. With spinner Anne Palmer taking 7 for 18, Australia were restricted to 138 in their second innings, and England knocked off the 32 needed to win for the loss of one wicket. Soon

Maclagan's opening partnership with Betty Snowball was being compared to that of Sutcliffe and Hobbs. The *Morning Post* waxed lyrical:

> *What matter that we lost, mere nervy men*
> *Since England's women now play England's game,*
> *Wherefore Immortal Wisden, take your pen*
> *And write MACLAGAN on the scroll of fame.*

In 1958 the International Women's Cricket Council was formed to co-ordinate women's cricket. Today there are nine women's Test teams: Australia; England; India; Ireland; New Zealand; Pakistan; South Africa; Sri Lanka; West Indies.

In addition, the following four countries have women's one-day teams: Denmark; Japan; Netherlands; Scotland.

THE HOLLYWOOD CRICKET CLUB

BORN IN 1863, the son of a Brighton doctor, Charles Aubrey Smith was educated at Charterhouse and Cambridge before going on to captain Sussex, where he earned the nickname of 'Round-the-Corner' Smith for his unorthodox bowling approach. W. G. Grace wrote of him: 'When Smith begins his run he is behind the umpire and out of sight of the batsman; and I can assure you it is rather startling when he suddenly appears at the bowling crease.' On other occasions he would start his run-up from the mid-off region. He was very much a law unto himself. He won one England cap – against South Africa in 1888 – but made his name as an actor, and at the age of sixty-three he moved to Hollywood, where he played the archetypal crusty Englishman in a host of films, including *The Prisoner of Zenda* and *The Life of a Bengal Lancer*.

Throughout his film career, however, he never lost his love of cricket, and set about re-creating the English village green in a corner of southern California. He bought five cartloads of English grass seed to plant a wicket and in 1933 officially opened the Hollywood Cricket Club in Griffith Park, Los Angeles. He wasted no time in recruiting major movie players. When a young Laurence Olivier booked into the Chateau Marmont Hotel to begin his first day as a film star in America, he found a note from Smith waiting for him: 'There will be nets tomorrow at 9 a.m. I trust I shall see you there.' Olivier obediently turned up in size 13 boots borrowed from Boris Karloff, who was himself no mean wicketkeeper. It was surely a test of any batsman's nerve to have Frankenstein's monster

breathing down his neck. Others who appeared in the regular Sunday afternoon fixtures included Errol Flynn, David Niven, George Coulouris and Basil Rathbone – all immaculately attired in harlequin caps and magenta, mauve and black striped blazers – while P. G. Wodehouse could often be found taking notes from the boundary. Smith remained an active member of the side in his seventies – taking fifty wickets a season – his eccentricity endearing him to all and sundry. In one match he was fielding in the slips when he spilled a catch. He immediately stopped the match and demanded that his butler be brought on to the pitch. 'Fetch me my glasses,' he bellowed. Several minutes later, with play still halted, the butler dutifully returned to the middle carrying the spectacles on a silver tray. A few balls later, Smith fumbled another slip catch and yelled at his butler: 'Damn fool, you brought me my reading glasses!' Right up until his death in 1948, cricket remained his abiding passion. At the club's AGM of May 1945 he spoke at length, not about victory in Europe, but of the more pressing concern of moles damaging the wicket.

The very Englishness of Sir Aubrey (he was knighted in 1944 for improving Anglo-American relations) attracted visiting international cricketers such as Gubby Allen, Denis Compton, Len Hutton and Godfrey Evans to the club. Although forced to move to the nearby town of Van Nuys in the 1960s, Hollywood CC continues to uphold Sir Aubrey's Edwardian values and fulfil his original aim of bringing a touch of much-needed civilization to the film colony.

THE TWO GRACES

IN AN ACCOUNT of an 1877 match in which Dr E. M. Grace, going in first, had made 200 not out and Dr A. Grace was left with 28 not out, *Wisden* observed: 'A doctor at the beginning, and a doctor at the end. Such is life.'

TEST BOWLERS WHO HAVE DISMISSED ALL ELEVEN BATSMEN

JIM LAKER (19 for 90) England v Australia, Old Trafford, 1956

SRINIVAS VENKATARAGHAVAN (12 for 152) India v New Zealand, Delhi, 1964–5

GEOFF DYMOCK (12 for 166) Australia v India, Kanpur, 1979–80

ABDUL QADIR (13 for 101) Pakistan v England, Lahore, 1987–8

WAQAR YOUNIS (12 for 130) Pakistan v New Zealand, Faisalabad, 1990–1

MUTTIAH MURALITHARAN (13 for 171) Sri Lanka v South Africa, Galle, 2000

ONE LEG v ONE ARM

TWELVE MEN with one leg played another twelve men with one arm at Islington in April 1867. The one-legged team made 89 and 132 (thanks in no small part to knocks of 46 and 62 from Birchmore), the one-armed replying with 143 and 59–9, so that the match ended in a draw.

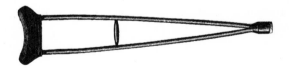

ALL OUT FOR 0

ON 13 AUGUST 1855, the Second Royal Surrey Militia met Shilinglee in Sussex at the seat of Earl Winterton. The scorecard of the Militia's first innings read:

Private Dudley	b Challen junior	0
Private Plumridge	b Heather	0
E. Hartnell, Esq	b Heather	0
A. Marshall, Esq	b Challen junior	0
Private Ayling	b Challen junior	0
Lt. Pontifex	b Heather	0
Corporal Heyes	b Heather	0
Lt. Ball	b Heather	0
Major Ridley	not out	0
Sgt Ayling	run out	0
Private Newberry	b Heather	0
Extras		0

Total 0

Apparently, Sergeant Ayling nearly spoilt the card by hitting the ball to cover point and setting off like a greyhound, only to be ordered by Major Ridley: 'Go back, Sergeant!' Obeying orders, Ayling pulled up sharp, fell flat on his face and was run out by 15 yards. The Militia did learn from the experience, however, and made 106 in their second innings.

On 22 June 1952, the Electrical Trades Commercial Travellers Association CC were routed by Surrey villagers Bookham for 0. To make matters worse, Bookham needed just one ball to overhaul their opponents' total, the first delivery of their reply sailing through for four byes.

FROM *The Young Cricketer's Tutor* BY JOHN NYREN (1833)

SON OF RICHARD NYREN, one of the driving forces of the famous Hambledon Club, John Nyren (1764–1837) was cricket's first real chronicler. Here he describes the style of Hambledon's renowned bowler, David Harris:

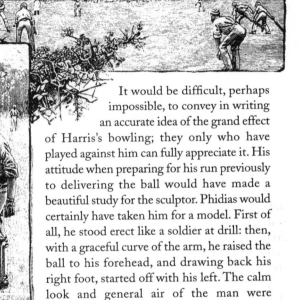

It would be difficult, perhaps impossible, to convey in writing an accurate idea of the grand effect of Harris's bowling; they only who have played against him can fully appreciate it. His attitude when preparing for his run previously to delivering the ball would have made a beautiful study for the sculptor. Phidias would certainly have taken him for a model. First of all, he stood erect like a soldier at drill: then, with a graceful curve of the arm, he raised the ball to his forehead, and drawing back his right foot, started off with his left. The calm look and general air of the man were uncommonly striking, and from this series of preparations he never deviated. I am sure that from this simple account of his manner, all my countrymen who were acquainted with his play will recall him to their minds. His mode of delivering the ball was very singular. He would bring it from under the arm by a twist, and nearly as high as his arm-pit, and with this action push it, as it were, from him. How it was the balls acquired the velocity they did by this mode of delivery I never could comprehend.

When he first joined the Hambledon Club, he was quite a raw countryman at cricket, and had very little to recommend him but his noble delivery. He was also very apt to give tosses. I have seen old Nyren scratch his head, and say – 'Harris would make the best bowler in England if he did not toss.' By continual practice, however, and following the advice of the old Hambledon players, he became as steady as could be wished; and in the prime of his playing very rarely indeed gave a toss, although his balls were pitched the full length. In bowling, he never stooped in the least in his delivery, but kept himself upright all the time. His balls were very little beholden to the ground when pitched; it was but a touch, and up again; and woe to the man who did not get in to block them, for they had such a peculiar curl, that they would grind his fingers against the bat: many a time have I seen the blood drawn in this way from a batter who was not up to the trick.

FIRST-CLASS HUNDREDS BY NUMBER ELEVEN BATSMEN

T. J. HASTINGS – 106* – Victoria v South Australia, 1902–3

A. FIELDER – 112* – Kent v Worcestershire, 1909

W. C. SMITH – 126 – MCC v Barbados, 1912–13

A. E. R. GILLIGAN – 101 – Cambridge University v Sussex, 1919

AHSAN-UL-HAQ – 100* – Muslims v Sikhs, 1923–4

S. N. BANERJEE – 121 – India v Surrey, 1946

T. P. B. SMITH – 163 – Essex v Derbyshire, 1947

MAQSOOD KUNDI – 109* – Muslim Commercial Bank v National Bank, 1981–2

G. B. STEVENSON – 115* Yorkshire v Warwickshire, 1982

S. VIDYUT – 115 – Tamil Nadu v Delhi, 2000–1

THE CRICKETER
WHO WAS KIDNAPPED

BORN IN GLOUCESTERSHIRE before emigrating to Australia, where he played for Victoria, Billy Midwinter was thus eligible to represent both countries. He had already made his Test debut for Australia against England when, in 1877, he decided to sail from Melbourne to become Gloucestershire's first professional. Although the Australians were touring England the following year, Gloucestershire's formidable captain W. G. Grace was under the distinct impression that Midwinter would be playing for the county instead. The Australians had other ideas, however, and selected him to play for them against Middlesex at Lord's on 20 June 1878. Due to open the batting, Midwinter was practising at the ground before the start of play when Grace and two Gloucestershire teammates – burly

wicketkeeper Arthur Bush and Grace's brother, E. M. – arrived and bundled him into a carriage bound for the Oval because Gloucestershire were a man short against Surrey. A posse of Australians, led by captain Dave Gregory, set off in hot pursuit with the intention of snatching back their man. This resulted in an angry altercation at the gates of the Oval where Grace called the Australians 'a damn lot of sneaks'. As usual, W. G. won the day, but Midwinter – torn between two suitors – could manage only 4 and 0 against Surrey as Gloucestershire slumped to their first defeat for two years. Worse still, he lost his place in the Australian team. A war of written words followed between Gloucestershire and the Australians before the tourists gained revenge later in the season when they visited Bristol and inflicted Gloucestershire's first ever home defeat. Conveniently, Midwinter was absent with a split thumb. In 1881 he switched international allegiance to England, thus becoming the first and only man to play for England against Australia and vice versa, but the following year he experienced another change of heart, and returned to Australia, for whom he played six more Tests. His last was in 1887, but three years later, aged thirty-nine, Billy Midwinter died in a Melbourne asylum after suffering mental problems following the death of his wife and children.

UMPIRES' CODE OF SIGNALS

TRADITION DICTATES that there are two umpires on a cricket field – one standing behind the stumps at the bowler's end, the other at square leg. However, there are four umpires in modern Test matches. In addition to the two on-field, a third umpire is responsible for adjudicating on decisions that are referred to television replays, while a fourth umpire looks after the match balls, takes out drinks to the on-field umpires, and arranges the umpires' travel and meals. Professional matches also have a match referee, who complements the role of the umpires. The match referee makes no decisions relevant to the outcome of the game, but enforces the ICC Cricket Code of Conduct, ensuring that the game is played in the proper manner.

Signals made by the umpire while the ball is in play:

Out: To denote that a batsman is out, the umpire raises the index finger above the head. If the appeal is turned down, the umpire calls 'Not out'.

No-ball: The umpire extends one arm horizontally.

Wide: Both arms are extended horizontally.

Dead ball: The umpire crosses and re-crosses the wrists below the waist.

Signals made by the umpire when the ball is dead:

Four: The umpire waves an arm from side to side, finishing with the arm across the chest. This signal varies considerably between umpires, from two short, restrained waves to elaborate movements worthy of an orchestra conductor.

Five: The arm is raised upwards with all fingers and thumb extended. Being something of a rarity, this signal is often accompanied by a bellow of 'Five!' to ensure that the scorers have got the message.

Six: Both arms are raised above the head.

Bye: The umpire raises an open hand above the head.

Leg-bye: The umpire touches a raised knee with the hand.

Short run: If either batsman turned without touching the popping crease, the umpire signals a 'short run' by bending one arm upwards and touching the nearer shoulder with the tips of the fingers.

Television replay: The umpire uses both hands to mime the shape of a TV screen.

New ball: The ball is held above the head.

Commencement of last hour: The umpire points to a raised wrist with the other hand.

Five penalty runs awarded to the batting side: In cases of extreme misconduct, the umpire may award five penalty runs. To award those runs to the batting side, the umpire repeatedly taps one shoulder with the opposite hand.

Five penalty runs awarded to the fielding side: One hand is placed on the opposite shoulder.

Revoke last signal: The umpire touches both shoulders, each with the opposite palm.

UMPIRES AND THEIR QUIRKS

DAVID SHEPHERD, who retired from umpiring at the end of the 2005 season, always gave a little hop when the score reached Nelson (111). The number is considered unlucky in cricket – possibly because it resembles a set of stumps without bails – and, according to superstition, the only way to prevent something bad happening on a Nelson number is to have no part of the body touching the ground. Shepherd adopted this routine as a Gloucestershire player and carried it through to umpiring. He has remarked: 'You could just lift your feet off the pavilion floor if you weren't in the middle, but if I was on the field of play I would hop or jump. When I took to umpiring, I thought I couldn't keep doing that, but a few friends urged me to carry on. Hardly anyone noticed at first but when I did my second Test, at Edgbaston in 1985, someone had written in to dear old Brian Johnston and said, "Watch this idiot when the score

gets on III." It did, I did my little jump and there was a titter in the crowd. I thought there must be a streaker on the field, but it was Brian telling the world – and the spectators were listening on their radios. I've been lumbered with it ever since.'

New Zealand's Brent 'Billy' Bowden has become a personality umpire through his use of imaginative signals. His trademark is his method of indicating 'out', which he does by curving his raised finger to resemble a hook – a gesture that has become known as the 'crooked finger of death'. For a 'six' he rises from a crouched position, finally propelling himself into the air, but leaving one leg on the ground while at the same time causing his two hands, which appear to be using sticks to play a drum, to rise with him. The end result is not dissimilar to the mating dance of a Bird of Paradise. Bowden's method for signalling 'four' has been likened to wiping breadcrumbs off a table, and his signal for 'leg byes' has been compared to a human pogo stick. In fact his unorthodox signals do not stem solely from eccentricity, but also from rheumatoid arthritis, the condition that forced him to give up his playing career in his early twenties. If he stands still for too long, he suffers acute pain, so his signals are a way of keeping in motion. Similarly, the curved finger developed because he finds it difficult to hold his finger straight. Arthritis also means that he can't hold items given to him by bowlers – such as sweaters and hats – which he therefore pushes up the front of his own sweater with the result that he often looks pregnant.

West Indian Steve Bucknor is another umpire with a distinctive mannerism. His nickname 'Slow Death' derives from the fact that he takes an eternity to raise the fatal finger to signal that a batsman is out.

Having previously worked on a racecourse, umpire Alec Skelding sometimes gave signals to the scorers in tic-tac. The short-sighted former Leicestershire fast bowler officiated in first-class matches from 1931 to 1958, but was considered too much of a maverick to officiate in a Test match. He used to carry a flask in his pocket, which, he insisted, 'keeps out the cold and helps me to see straight'. England batsman Joe Hardstaff recalled going out to bat and being told by Skelding that there would be no lbw decisions because he was wearing his reading glasses by mistake. Skelding's poor eyesight made him the butt of various remarks, usually jovial but occasionally more caustic. During the 1948 Australian tour, Skelding had just turned down a confident appeal when a dog ran to the field. The tourists' Sid Barnes captured the animal and carried it to Skelding with the comment: 'Now all you want is a white stick.'

The escapades of Harold 'Dickie' Bird have passed into cricketing folklore. Many have been told too often to warrant repeating here, but it is worth recalling the incident at the 1983 Trent Bridge Test between England and New Zealand, when poor old Dickie was left hopping with indignation after Ian Botham had sprinkled some Chinese crackers behind the stumps at the Radcliffe Road End. Bird remembered: 'With every step I took there was a loud explosion which had me jumping about like a cat on a hot tin roof.'

Throughout his thirty-three years as an umpire, Frank Chester kept the same six stones as counters. The stones, which he had dug up from his garden, became a familiar prop on the English county circuit, particularly as he used to toss them in the air in an exaggerated manner to mark each delivery. During the winter he lovingly stored them in a matchbox for safe keeping. Chester had taken up umpiring after the loss of an arm in the First World War curtailed his playing career, and he performed his duties with the help of an artificial arm. Unfortunately, during a match against Sussex, Surrey's Freddie Brown drove a half-volley straight back into Chester's false arm, the force knocking it out of its socket. There was an awkward silence as the arm lay on the grass, but Chester calmly left the field, had the arm refitted and returned to the action. When he resumed his position, however, instead of adopting his customary crouching position almost at eye level with the bails at the bowler's end, he made a point of standing several yards behind them.

Nor could anybody doubt Harry Bagshaw's dedication to duty. In accordance with his wishes, the former Derbyshire opening batsman was buried in 1927 dressed in his umpire's coat and clutching a cricket ball. His headstone depicted a set of broken stumps, dislodged bails and an umpire's hand with the index finger raised skywards, signalling symbolically, 'Out.'

SLOWEST INDIVIDUAL BATTING IN TESTS

Runs	Mins	
0	101	GEOFF ALLOTT (New Zealand v South Africa, Auckland, 1998–9)
5	102	NAWAB OF PATAUDI JNR (India v England, Bombay, 1972–3)
6	106	DAMIEN MARTYN (Australia v South Africa, Sydney, 1993–4)
7	123	GEOFF MILLER (England v Australia, Melbourne, 1978–9)
9	132	RAJESH CHAUHAN (India v Sri Lanka, Ahmedabad, 1993–4)
10*	133	GODFREY EVANS (England v Australia, Adelaide, 1946–7)
14*	165	DANNY MORRISON (New Zealand v England, Auckland, 1996–7)
18	194	WILLIAM PLAYLE (New Zealand v England, Headingley, 1958)
19	217	MARTIN CROWE (New Zealand v Sri Lanka, Colombo, 1983–4)
25	242	DANNY MORRISON (New Zealand v Pakistan, Faisalabad, 1990–1)

A LOAD OF OLD BAILS

EACH BAIL is four and three-eighths inches long and should not project more than half an inch above the stumps. The wicket is 'down' if either of the bails is dislodged from the stumps by the ball or by the batsman (with his bat, body or clothing). If the wind is very strong, the two captains may agree, with the umpires' consent, to dispense with the bails altogether.

In the early days of the single bail and even after the introduction of the third stump (which needed two bails), manufacturers often supplied the bail in one piece, leaving umpires or players to snap it approximately in half. As a result the bails were often splintered and this, combined with the fact that they were generously coated in varnish, which would melt in the sun, meant that they were not always dislodged when the ball hit the wicket.

AN ECCENTRIC XI

- **GEORGE GUNN**, who scored over 35,000 runs for Nottinghamshire from 1902 to 1932, was a stickler for taking lunch on time. In a game against Hampshire at Southampton, he set off for the pavilion at 1.30 p.m., only to be informed by the umpire that lunch was being taken at two o'clock instead. Gunn calmly returned to the crease, deliberately allowed the next ball to hit his wicket, tucked his bat under his arm and announced as he departed, 'I take my lunch at 1.30.'

- **ERNEST KILLICK**, who played for Sussex between 1892 and 1913, was so fond of music that when the band struck up a waltz at a county match he began dancing at the crease. He was immediately bowled with his feet nowhere near the pitch of the ball.

- Throughout his forty-three-year career as player and umpire, Gloucestershire's JACK CRAPP always wore the same pair of cricket boots.

- After being bowled by Derbyshire's Ian Buxton in 1968, the volatile MAJID JAHANGIR of Glamorgan and Pakistan stormed off to the pavilion and sawed his bat in half.

- LIONEL, LORD TENNYSON, grandson of the poet, captained Hampshire in the years following the First World War, nobly assisted by his personal manservant Walter Livsey, the county's wicketkeeper. Tennyson's aristocratic approach extended to issuing instructions to his batsmen in the middle by telegram. One player, struggling to lay bat on ball, was surprised to see a boy in a blue uniform trotting out with a small envelope. It was a telegram from Tennyson in the pavilion, asking the recipient what he thought his bat was for.

- Omitted from the Australian Test team, SIDNEY BARNES asked whether he could be twelfth man for New South Wales against South Australia at the Adelaide Oval in 1953. At the drinks interval Barnes strode out to the square dressed as a butler carrying a tray with a scent spray, portable radio and cigars, which he then offered to players and umpires alike.

- Gloucestershire wicketkeeper JACK RUSSELL survived England overseas tours on thirty cups of tea a day and a diet of baked beans. He considered Weetabix inedible unless it had been soaked in the milk for exactly twelve minutes.

- BOBBY PEEL of Yorkshire and England was just about the best slow left-arm bowler of his day. However, his career effectively ended when he turned up drunk for the match with Middlesex at Bramall Lane, Sheffield, in 1897. The hapless Peel had to be escorted bodily from the field by his captain,

Lord Hawke, after allegedly bowling at the sightscreen in the mistaken belief that it was a Middlesex batsman.

- Another heavy drinker was Derbyshire fast bowler **BILL BESTWICK**. Despite being allocated a minder by the county, Bestwick frequently managed to give him the slip. A report of the 1921 fixture with Gloucestershire stated: 'Bestwick occasionally suffered from a "thirst" and as a result was unable to bowl or field much in Gloucestershire's second innings.' The following year he turned up drunk at Worcester and proceeded to barrack his own team from the stand.

- Essex slow bowler **RAY EAST** used to entertain the crowd by acting like a *Thunderbirds* puppet. Ever the improviser, he was playing at Scarborough one afternoon while a mock gun battle was being fought in a nearby park. As East ran up to bowl, the sound of cannon fire reverberated across the ground, at which point he collapsed in front of the umpire as if he had been shot.

- **LESLIE O'BRIEN 'CHUCK' FLEETWOOD-SMITH** was an Australian left-arm spinner, who represented his country on ten occasions between 1935 and 1938. As he came in to bowl he used to do elaborate bird impressions, his favourites being the screech of the magpie and the whoop of the whipbird.

ENGLAND TEST PLAYERS WHO SCORED A CENTURY IN THEIR TEST-MATCH DEBUT

W. G. GRACE 152 v Australia, Oval, 1880
K. S. RANJITSINHJI 154* v Australia, Old Trafford, 1896
PELHAM WARNER 132* v South Africa, Johannesburg, 1898–9
REGINALD FOSTER 287 v Australia, Sydney, 1903–4
GEORGE GUNN 119 v Australia, Sydney, 1907–8
NAWAB OF PATAUDI SNR 102 v Australia, Sydney, 1932–3
BRYAN VALENTINE 136 v India, Bombay, 1933–4
PAUL GIBB 106 v South Africa, Johannesburg, 1938–9
STEWART GRIFFITH 140 v West Indies, Port of Spain, 1947–8
PETER MAY 138 v South Africa, Headingley, 1951
ARTHUR MILTON 104* v New Zealand, Headingley, 1958
JOHN HAMPSHIRE 107 v West Indies, Lord's, 1969
FRANK HAYES 106* v West Indies, Oval, 1973
GRAHAM THORPE 114* v Australia, Trent Bridge, 1993
ANDREW STRAUSS 112 v New Zealand, Lord's, 2004

A BRIEF ENCOUNTER

AFTER GETTING THE WICKET of Craig McDermott in the 1991 Perth Test, Phil Tufnell heard the Australian fast bowler snarl, 'You've got to bat on this in a minute. Hospital food suit you?' When Tufnell nervously came out to bat with England in disarray, he faced a monster of a ball from Merv Hughes that reared up from a length, caught him on the top of the thumb and went through for a catch. To Tufnell's horror, the umpire seemed on the point of rejecting the appeal, so Tufnell wailed, 'Ow, my thumb. I think you've broken my thumb.' The umpire took the hint and raised his finger, allowing Tufnell to return to the safety of the pavilion 'not a moment too soon'.

MOST BALLS BOWLED
IN A TEST INNINGS

588 Sonny Ramadhin (98–35–179–2), West Indies v England,
      Edgbaston, 1957
571 Tom Veivers (95.1–36–155–3), Australia v England, Old Trafford,
      1964
552 Alf Valentine (92–49–140–3), West Indies v England, Trent Bridge,
      1950
522 Chuck Fleetwood-Smith (87–11–298–1), Australia v England,
      Oval, 1938
512 Fazal Mahmood (85.2–20–247–2), Pakistan v W. Indies, Kingston,
      1957–8
510 Bill O'Reilly (85–26–178–3), Australia v England, Oval, 1938
504 Haseeb Ahsan (84–19–202–6), Pakistan v India, Madras, 1960–1
492 Vinoo Mankad (82–17–228–5), India v West Indies, Kingston,
      1952–3
488 Sonny Ramadhin (81.2–25–135–5), W. Indies v England, Trent
      Bridge, 1950
486 George Geary (81–36–105–5), England v Australia, Melbourne,
      1928–9

JOHN WISDEN

JOHN WISDEN was born in 1826, the son of a Brighton builder. His
father died when he was still a boy and young John went to live, as a
pot-boy, with Tom Box, who taught him the game of cricket.
Wisden was described in chronicles of the time as 'a hungry-looking
lad, glad of one's sixpence for his trouble', but by 1845 he had been
chosen to play for Sussex. Although only 5 feet 4 inches tall and
weighing 7 stone, he became a feared fast bowler known as the
'Little Wonder' and averaged 225 wickets a season for twelve years.

In 1850, he clean-bowled all ten wickets in the second innings of a North v South match. He went on to own a tobacconist and sports equipment store in London's Leicester Square, a business in which his chief rival was Lillywhite Brothers & Co of Islington who, since 1849, had issued the *Young Cricketer's Guide* at 18d a copy. Seeing the value of such a publication for advertising purposes, Wisden decided to produce his own, and in 1864 he launched the *Wisden Cricketers' Almanack*. The first issue contained 112 pages and sold for 1s.

CRICKET AND WAR

IT IS ONE OF LIFE'S INCONGRUITIES that a game devised for the village green and a round of cucumber sandwiches should also be played in war zones more readily associated with a round of machine-gun fire. That cricket can somehow make life seem normal even in abnormal situations was illustrated once again in the summer of 2005 when British and Australian troops in Iraq conducted their own Desert Ashes series, played at the same time as the real

Ashes were being fought over back in England. The Royal Engineers flattened an area of Camp Smitty in the south-east of the country and laid down green matting for the wicket. Despite searing, 50-degree heat, dust storms and the frequent landings and departures of helicopters at the base, the 25-overs-a-side matches were keenly contested, particularly by the Australians, who swept to victory in the first four Tests. Wearing green and gold uniforms donated by the Australia Cricket Board, the Aussies set the tone for the series in the opening match, crushing England by 119 runs. For Glenn McGrath, read Capt. Nathan Schurmann, who snapped up 4 for 17 in just four overs.

Such wartime pursuits are nothing new of course. Before the Battle of Waterloo in 1815, officers of the Brigade of Guards played cricket – the first recorded instance of cricket in Belgium. During a short break in the Battle of Vermelles in 1915, the poet Robert Graves played cricket using a rafter as a bat, a ball made from rifle rags, and a wicket simulated by a birdcage housing a dead parrot.

In the same year Australian
troops conducted a cricket match
on Shell Green in Gallipoli just
before the evacuation, as part of the
highly successful operation to convince
the Turks that everything was normal,
and that the British and Anzac forces were
still occupying their positions on the peninsula
in strength. The Great War ultimately claimed
the lives of many first-class cricketers, but the risk
to life and limb did not prevent them leaving to serve
their country. When Leicestershire played at
Northampton in August 1914, A. T. Sharp, having made 2 in the
first innings, was listed on the scorecard for the second innings as
'absent . . . o'. On the evening of 4 August, Sharp had packed his

bags in mid-match and gone to join his regiment. Among those who served was the great Jack Hobbs, although it is said that officers were under orders to keep him as far away from the action as possible lest England should lose one of its sporting heroes. The Germans were all too aware of the propaganda value of the death of a famous cricketer to the extent that when W. G. Grace expired of natural causes on 23 October 1915, they tried to claim him as an air-raid victim.

A special match was staged between an English Army XI and an Australian Army XI at Lord's in 1917. *Wisden* reported: 'In the bright sunshine on the 14th of July, Lord's ground looked quite its old self. The public mustered in surprisingly large numbers, the pleasure felt in seeing even a one-day match of some general interest being very keen. So good was the attendance and sale of tickets beforehand that St Dunstan's Hostel for blinded soldiers and sailors benefited to the extent of about £620. Two capital sides were got together, the English team being composed entirely of men who before the War had taken part in first-class cricket.' An England team including Plum Warner, Percy Fender, Johnny Douglas and Patsy Hendren won by five wickets, although *Wisden* noted that a lack of match practice made both sets of batsmen over-cautious.

Cricket was played more regularly during the Second World War, with select matches taking place at Lord's between air raids. The indomitable spirit shown by the cricketing fraternity was exemplified by the following notice pinned to the gates of a South Coast cricket ground shortly after a German bombing raid: 'Local cricketers are as pleased as you. Each peardrop which fell on this ground saved lives and property. We shall carry on. Nothing which falls from the skies will deter us, except RAIN.'

And cricket actually served as the peacemaker during a dispute between two warring tribes on the Afghan–Indian border in the 1930s. In a flash of inspiration a British officer arranged a cricket match between the opposing factions. Honour was satisfied by the game, and bloodletting averted.

TEST PLAYERS
WHO HAVE REPRESENTED
TWO COUNTRIES

AMIR ELAHI (India 1947; Pakistan 1952)
JOHN FERRIS (Australia 1887–90; England 1892)
SIMPSON GUILLEN (West Indies 1951–2; New Zealand 1956)
GUL MOHAMMAD (India 1946–52; Pakistan 1956)
FRANK HEARNE (England 1889; South Africa 1892–6)
ABDUL KARDAR (India 1946; Pakistan 1952–8)
BILLY MIDWINTER (Australia 1877–87; England 1881–2)
FRANK MITCHELL (England 1899; South Africa 1912)
BILLY MURDOCH (Australia 1877–90; England 1892)
NAWAB OF PATAUDI SNR (England 1932–4; India 1946)
ATHANASIOS TRAICOS (South Africa 1970; Zimbabwe 1992–3)
ALBERT TROTT (Australia 1895; England 1899)
KEPLER WESSELS (Australia 1982–5; South Africa 1992–4)
SAMMY WOODS (Australia 1888; England 1896)

A TALE OF
FOUR WICKETKEEPERS

BATTING IN THE FIRST TEST between England and New Zealand at Lord's in 1986, England wicketkeeper Bruce French was hit on the head by a ball from Richard Hadlee and had to retire hurt. With French unable to field in New Zealand's reply, teammate Bill Athey took his place behind the stumps for a couple of overs but then, with the agreement of visiting captain Jeremy Coney, England dragged forty-five-year-old Bob Taylor from a hospitality tent and persuaded him to pad up again for old time's sake. Although he had been retired from the game for two years, Taylor turned back the clock and kept immaculately for the rest of the second day before making way for a more conventional substitute – Hampshire's Bobby Parks – the following morning. French was fit enough to return for the last ball of the first innings and the whole of the second, but the match goes down in history as the only Test in which a team has used four different wicketkeepers.

The Batsman
Who Wore Inflatable Pads

A PATRON OF THE GAME between the wars, East Midlands furniture magnate Sir Julien Cahn took his team of country-house cricketers on tours to Jamaica, New Zealand, North and South America and the Far East. Sir Julien himself had unusually fragile bones and, in order to protect his legs, commissioned a pair of inflatable batting pads, which were inflated with a bicycle pump by his chauffeur before each innings. Although they may have looked cumbersome, they helped the scoreboard tick along nicely, as any ball that pitched off-line was invariably shinned away by Sir Julien for leg byes. On the downside, however, they were uncomfortable to walk in for any distance, as a result of which Sir Julien often summoned a bath chair to convey him from the pavilion to the wicket and back again.

CROSSED WIRES

TV INTERVIEWER: Do you feel that the selectors and yourself have been vindicated by this result?

MIKE GATTING: I don't think the press are vindictive. They can write what they want.

FROM *Preamble to the Laws of Cricket –*
The Spirit of Cricket (2000 Code)

5. **It is against the Spirit of the Game**

- To dispute an umpire's decision by word, action or gesture.
- To direct abusive language towards an opponent or umpire.
- To indulge in cheating or any sharp practice, for instance:
  - To appeal knowing that the batsman is not out.
  - To advance towards an umpire in an aggressive manner when appealing.
  - To seek to distract an opponent either verbally or by harassment with persistent clapping or unnecessary noise under the guise of enthusiasm and motivation of one's own side.

CRICKETERS' NICKNAMES

ALTHOUGH THE OCCASIONAL 'Warney', 'Harmy' and 'Straussy' manage to slip through the net, thankfully most cricketers put a little more effort and imagination into thinking up appropriate nicknames for their teammates.

Physical characteristics are the most obvious source for nicknames. So Glenn McGrath is 'Pigeon' on account of his long, thin legs and the way he walks; Paul Adams is 'Frog in a blender' for his bizarre bowling action; Keith Fletcher was 'Gnome' for his hunched batting style; to his dismay Ashley Giles has been christened 'Wheelie Bin' by Henry Blofeld because of his rolling gait when he runs up to bowl; Robin Smith was known universally as 'Judge' because his hair looked like a judge's wig; Ian Botham was 'Guy the Gorilla' or 'Beefy', and Graham McKenzie was 'Garth' because of their powerful physiques; at the other end of the fitness scale Colin

Milburn was 'Ollie' because he resembled Oliver Hardy, while the portly Inzamam-ul-Haq is 'Potato'; the gangling builds of former Australian Test player Hunter Hendry and West Indian paceman Joel Garner earned them the nicknames of 'Stork' and 'Big Bird' respectively; Gilbert Jessop was 'The Croucher' because of his batting stance; David Lloyd was called 'Bumble' apparently because his nose resembled those of the 1950s children's TV characters the Bumblies; and Michael Vaughan is 'Virgil' because of a perceived similarity to the clean-cut hero from *Thunderbirds*.

Some nicknames owe more to personality quirks. Derek Randall was named 'Arkle' after the famous racehorse partly because he was so jumpy in the field; Marcus Trescothick is 'Banger' because he loves sausages; South African Hugh Tayfield was called 'Toey' due to his habit of stubbing his toe into the ground before bowling a ball or receiving one; Charles Thornton was known as 'Buns' from his days at Eton where he once held a high catch while eating a bun; Trevor Bailey was 'Barnacle' for his tenacity at the crease; and

Phil Tufnell was known as 'The Cat', not for his supreme athleticism, but because he slept through his twelfth-man duties for Middlesex at Headingley in 1988.

Others take their nicknames from superlative descriptions. Hence 'The Rawalpindi Express' (Shoaib Akhtar), 'White Lightning' (Allan Donald), 'Whispering Death' (Michael Holding), 'Super Cat' (Clive Lloyd), 'The Turbanator' (Harbhajan Singh), 'Demon' (Fred Spofforth), 'Deadly' (Derek Underwood), 'Little Master' (Sachin Tendulkar), 'The Sultans of Reverse Swing' (Wasim Akram and Waqar Younis), and 'The Golden Eagle' (Colin Bland, because the South African swooped in the field to run out opposing batsmen).

Then there are puns taken from players' names – 'Pistol' (Paul Reiffel), 'Freddie' (Andrew Flintoff), 'Dazzler' (Darren Gough), 'Dizzy' (Jason Gillespie), 'Swampy' (Geoff Marsh), 'Grizzly' (Chris Adams), 'Tiger' (Dennis Lillee), and the Sussex pair from the 1960s, Tony and Michael Buss, known affectionately as 'Omni' and 'Trolley'. A handful are initial-based. V. V. S. Laxman is considered 'Very Very Special', while England's J. W. H. T. Douglas was christened 'Johnny Won't Hit Today' by the Australians because of his defensive batting.

Finally, there are the more obscure nicknames. Mark Waugh was called 'Afghanistan' in the early days of his career when he was overlooked in favour of twin brother Steve and was thus considered to be the 'forgotten Waugh'; rugged Australian Ken Mackay was ironically nicknamed 'Slasher' because that was exactly what he *didn't* do while batting; and Yorkshire and Hampshire opening bowler Peter Hartley was known as 'Daisy' because, when it came to swinging the ball, some days he does, some days he doesn't.

WARWICKSHIRE MUGS

ASHLEY GILES acquired a new nickname in 2004 after the writing on souvenir mugs at the Warwickshire CCC shop at Edgbaston erroneously described him as the King of Spain instead of the King of Spin!

BATSMEN DISMISSED IN TESTS
MOST TIMES BY THE SAME BOWLER

19 Mike Atherton (England) by Glenn McGrath (Australia)

18 Arthur Morris (Australia) by Alec Bedser (England)

17 Mike Atherton (England) by Curtly Ambrose (West Indies)

17 Mike Atherton (England) by Courtney Walsh (West Indies)

16 Graham Gooch (England) by Malcolm Marshall (West Indies)

15 Mark Waugh (Australia) by Curtly Ambrose (West Indies)

15 Thomas Hayward (England) by Hugh Trumble (Australia)

15 Ian Healy (Australia) by Courtney Walsh (West Indies)

14 David Gower (England) by Geoff Lawson (Australia)

14 Brian Lara (West Indies) by Glenn McGrath (Australia)

14 Dick Lilley (England) by Monty Noble (Australia)

14 Alec Stewart (England) by Shane Warne (Australia)

AN EPIGRAM

IN 1751 Frederick, Prince of Wales (eldest son of George II), died at the age of forty-four, supposedly from an abscess caused by a blow to the head from a cricket ball. An anonymous epigram recorded his passing:

> *Here lies poor Fred, who was alive and is dead.*
> *Had it been his father, I had much rather,*
> *Had it been his sister, nobody would have missed her,*
> *Had it been his brother, still better than another,*
> *Had it been the whole generation, so much better for the nation,*
> *But since it is Fred, who was alive and is dead,*
> *There is no more to be said!*

STRANGE OCCURRENCES
ON THE FIELD OF PLAY

- Bowling for Pakistan against Somerset at Taunton in July 1954, Hanif Mohammad delivered four balls right-handed and two left-handed in one over before lunch, a feat he repeated after tea.

- In 1996, twins Chris and James Sell both dislocated a shoulder playing in the same match for Brighton College against Old Brightonians.

- D. Walker of Middlesex was bowling against Nottinghamshire at Trent Bridge in 1884 when his hat fell off. Notts opener William Scotton drove the ball back, but the hat intercepted it.

- When Sussex's Ian Thomson hit a delivery from the West Indies' Alf Valentine to square leg, a black dog ran on to the Hove pitch, picked up the ball and carried it over the boundary, hotly pursued by fielders and umpires. Four runs were credited to Thomson.

- In 1969, John Inverarity of Western Australia was bowled by a delivery from South Australia's Greg Chappell that hit a swallow in mid-air and was deflected on to the stumps. The umpires signalled a no-ball and Inverarity, who had yet to score, went on to make 89.

- Playing against Worcestershire in 1955, Sussex's Robin Marlar bowled three consecutive deliveries in one over with three different balls. The first two had been driven out of the ground and declared 'lost' as a result of big hits by Robert Broadbent.

- During a County Championship game between Leicester-shire and Lancashire in 1975, Leicestershire's substitute wicketkeeper Barry Dudleston stumped Lancashire batsman David Lloyd, only to see the bails jump up and miraculously land back in their sockets. Lloyd made the most of his fortuitous reprieve by going on to compile a century.

- After Hampshire's George Brown had flung himself into the path of a Jack Hobbs off-drive, the ball was prised from his fingers to reveal that the manufacturer's gilt trademark and address (in reverse) were embossed upon his palm.

- In a 1990 Victoria country fixture against Macleod, the Banyale batsmen ran 17 after Garry Chapman hit the ball into 10-inch-high long grass at mid-wicket.

- In 2003, when Gareth Lewis hit a six during a game at Nawton, North Yorkshire, the ball landed in a car radiator grille, continued up the A170 and ended up in a garage at Kirkbymoorside, three and a half miles away.

- Former Pakistan Test player Parvez Mir was disciplined by the Carrow club of Norfolk in 1995 for interrupting his bowling in the middle of an over to take a call from his fiancée on his mobile phone.

- During the second innings of the Rugby v Marlborough public-school match at Lord's in July 1886, Mr C. W. Bengough, the Rugby captain, was allowed by the umpires to bowl successive overs from each end. During this time he had his opposite number, Mr S. Kitcat, caught at cover point. Although the mistake was pointed out and Bengough was not allowed to bowl again in the match, it was an unlucky break for Kitcat as the umpires refused to let him resume his innings, ruling that he had been fairly caught.

- The history of Radley College tells how W. E. W. Collins dismissed three men with one delivery. 'The first victim was hit on the thumb and was led out bleeding profusely, his colleague fainted and the next man in decided not to bat.'

- In the first Test between England and India at Old Trafford in 1974, Madan Lal was bowled spectacularly by Mike Hendrick. His off and leg stumps were knocked out of the ground but, bizarrely enough, the middle stump remained standing.

- Batting for Somerset against Nottinghamshire at Taunton in 1930, G. Hunt was so troubled by Bill Voce's vicious in-swingers that he changed to batting left-handed against the Notts fast bowler. He continued to bat in his usual right-handed manner against the other bowlers.

- When E. W. Dillon bowled his first over for Kent against Surrey at the Oval in 1902, every ball was hit for a single down to Cuthbert Burnup fielding at deep third-man.

MINOR LEAGUE CRICKET BOWLERS WHO TOOK ALL 10 WICKETS FOR 0 RUNS

A. DARTNELL (Broad Green v Thornton Heath, 1867)

R. T. P. TEARNE (Pershore v Swinden's XI, 1879)

J. COTTRELL (St Benedict's v Pupil Teachers Assoc, Liverpool, 1885)

F. RAE (Alliance v Granville, Drayton Park, 1885)

J. TUNE (Cliffe v Eastrington, 1922)

S. TUCKER (Homedale School v Horley Council School, Reigate, 1924)

G. ALLEN (Bittern v Someville, Victoria, 1946–7)

D. USHERWOOD (St George's Harpenden Under-12s, 1948)

C. G. WOODROW (Bournemouth Electric v Cranborne, 1961)

J. BURR (Strathmore v Strathmore North, Victoria, 1962–3)

N. DOHERTY (Panania Easts v Regent's Park, Sydney, 1965–6)

D. POOLE (Taunton School Under-13 v Glen Eyre, 1966)

D. NORQUAY (Seaforth v Pittwater, Sydney, 1966–7)

R. MORGAN (Beachport Colts v Cellulose, Millicent, South Australia, 1968–9)

A. KELLY (Bishop Auckland v Newton Aycliffe, Durham, 1994)

EMMA LIDDELL (Metropolitan East v Metropolitan West, Penrith, 1995–6)

D. MORTON (Bayside Muddies v Ranatungas, Brisbane, 1998–9)

In October 1825, five gentlemen of Kent played five gentlemen of Sussex at Newenden. The scorecard read:

KENT	FIRST INNINGS	
Mr G. Tolhurst	b Warner	o
Mr T. Ayerst	b Warner	o
Mr W. Hunson	c Warner	o
Mr R. Levett	b Warner	o
Mr S. Maynard	lbw	o

SUSSEX	FIRST INNINGS	
Mr J. Furner	b Ayerst	o
Mr T. Edwards	b Ayerst	o
Mr T. Coppinger	b Ayerst	o
Mr R. Moore	b Ayerst	o
Mr T. Warner	b Ayerst	o

The advent of nightfall prevented the second innings being played.

No escape

IT IS RUMOURED that some club cricketers play the game simply in order to get away from their wives for a few hours, but there was no escape for one poor soul taking part in a match at Howick, South Africa, in 1958. His wife telephoned the ground and insisted on speaking to him even though he was batting at the time. Consequently the match was held up while he dashed to the pavilion to deal with what was obviously a family crisis. Indeed it was: she wanted to know what he had done with the soap!

What the Club Cricketer Says and What He Really Means

He says: I don't mind where I bat.
He means: As long as it's in the top five.

He says: I've had a fair season with the bat.
He means: I managed to get into double figures on a couple of occasions.

He says: I don't mind turning my arm over if needs be.
He means: I couldn't bowl much worse than this lot.

He says: I had the batsman in two minds.
He means: He didn't know whether to hit me for a four or a six.

He says: Did you spot my slower ball?
He means: As it disappeared over the sightscreen.

He says: Yes, yes, come on, a single, no, wait, go back, oh bad luck, sorry.
He means: That'll teach you to flirt with my wife.

He says: Jolly good knock, old man.
He means: Lucky bastard! Should have been out at least six times.

He says: I'm best in the deep.
He means: Where I can get some peace.

He says: Sorry, skipper, I didn't pick it up out of the trees.
He means: I was daydreaming about that blonde near the long-off boundary.

He says: I played too late.
He means: I missed it.

He says: He's turning them a lot.
He means: I missed it.

SLEDGING IN PRINT

If any of our batsmen get out to [Ashley] Giles
in the Tests they should go and hang themselves.
Australian TERRY ALDERMAN, *2005*

Jason Gillespie is a thirty-year-old
in a thirty-six-year-old body.
BOB WILLIS

At best, his action is suspicious.
At worst it belongs in a darts tournament.
MICHAEL PARKINSON *joins the debate*
on Muttiah Muralitharan

He can be so rude to people that sometimes
you just want to punch his lights out.
MARK NICHOLAS
on co-commentator Geoffrey Boycott

Illy [Ray Illingworth] had the man-management skills
of Basil Fawlty.
DARREN GOUGH

[Ian] Botham's idea of team spirit and motivation was to
squirt a water pistol at someone and then go and get pissed.
RAY ILLINGWORTH

He crossed the line between eccentricity and idiocy
far too often for someone who was supposed
to be running English cricket.
IAN BOTHAM *on Ted Dexter*

Why is [Phil] Tufnell the most popular man in the team?
Is it the Manuel factor, in which the most helpless member
of the cast is most affectionately identified with?
MIKE BREARLEY

He looks and bats like a librarian: a prodder and nudger
with a virile bottom hand that works the ball to the on side
and a top hand for keeping the other glove on.
MIKE SELVEY
on New Zealand batsman Bert Vance

Richard Hadlee has the appearance of a rickety church
steeple and a severe manner which suggests that women
are not likely to be ordained yet.
PETER ROEBUCK

[Angus] Fraser's approach to the wicket currently resembles
someone who has his braces caught in the sightscreen.
MARTIN JOHNSON

A 1914 biplane tied up with elastic bands
trying vainly to take off.
FRANK KEATING
assessing the run-up of Bob Willis

His mincing approach resembled someone in high heels
and a panty-girdle running after a bus.
MARTIN JOHNSON
describing Merv Hughes' run-up

There's only one head bigger than Tony Greig's
and that's Birkenhead.
FRED TRUEMAN

No-Balls and Googlies

The only time an Australian walks
is when his car runs out of petrol.
<small>BARRY RICHARDS</small>

The traditional dress of the Australian cricketer
is the baggy green cap on the head and the chip
on the shoulder. Both are ritualistically assumed.
<small>SIMON BARNES</small>

THE HOME OF CRICKET

ALTHOUGH BORN IN YORKSHIRE, Thomas Lord learned his cricket in Norfolk before moving to London around 1778. In those days the main cricket ground in the capital was situated next to White Conduit House, a tavern in Islington. The Cricket Club (the forerunner of the MCC) rented the ground but were on the lookout for new premises, and so in 1786 it was suggested to Lord, who worked in a general capacity for the club as well as operating a thriving wine business, that if he were to open a private ground the club would move its allegiance from Islington. The following year Lord took a lease on a field in Marylebone (near Dorset Square) and prepared the ground for cricket. He and the club stayed there until 1809, when Lord, learning that the land was required for building, opened a second ground half a mile to the north-west. However, in 1813 it emerged that the Regents Canal was to be constructed through the new site, forcing Lord to move once again – this time a quarter of a mile away to a site off St John's Wood Road. This third ground is the location of the present-day Lord's. The rent was £100 per annum, but the grand opening in 1814 nearly had to be postponed after the landlady of the nearby public house accidentally sparked a gunpowder explosion that seriously injured herself, her sister and four young girls. The incident cast a shadow over the first game played there, in which the Marylebone Cricket

[134]

Club (as it was now known) defeated Hertfordshire by an innings and 27 runs.

In 1825, Lord planned to build houses on a large area of the ground but was bought out by William Ward for £5,000. Ward was already assured of a place in Lord's history, having scored 278 for the MCC against Norfolk five years earlier – an individual record for the ground that would stand until 1925, when Percy Holmes hit 315 not out for Yorkshire against Middlesex. Incidentally, Edward Budd had the distinction of hitting the first century at Lord's, in 1816.

The Lord's of the nineteenth century bore little similarity to today's ground. For a start, there were two ponds – one in front of the present Mound Stand and the other at the west end of the ground – where one of the early groundsmen learned to swim. Sheep used to be herded in before a game to nibble the outfield and, when the cricket season finished, pony races were held. But at least Lord's didn't have the macabre feel of the Oval, where executions sometimes took place.

THE WORLD'S OLDEST TEST GROUNDS
(featuring the date of the first Test played there)

MELBOURNE CRICKET GROUND, Melbourne, Australia,
15 March 1877
THE OVAL, London, England, 6 September 1880
SYDNEY CRICKET GROUND, Sydney, Australia, 17 February 1882

OLD TRAFFORD, Manchester, England, 10 July 1884
LORD'S, London, England, 21 July 1884
ADELAIDE OVAL, Adelaide, Australia, 12 December 1884
SAHARA OVAL ST GEORGE'S, Port Elizabeth, South Africa,
12 March 1889
NEWLANDS, Cape Town, South Africa, 25 March 1889
OLD WANDERERS NO 1 GROUND, Johannesburg,
South Africa, 2 March 1896
TRENT BRIDGE, Nottingham, England, 1 June 1899
HEADINGLEY, Leeds, England, 29 June 1899
EDGBASTON, Birmingham, England, 29 May 1902
BRAMALL LANE, Sheffield, England, 3 July 1902
LORD'S NO. 1 GROUND, Durban, South Africa, 21 January 1910
KINGSMEAD, Durban, South Africa, 18 January 1923
EXHIBITION GROUND, Brisbane, Australia, 30 November 1928

JADE STADIUM, Christchurch, New Zealand, 10 January 1930
KENSINGTON OVAL, Bridgetown, Barbados, 11 January 1930
BASIN RESERVE, Wellington, New Zealand, 24 January 1930
QUEEN'S PARK OVAL, Port of Spain, Trinidad and Tobago,
1 February 1930
EDEN PARK, Auckland, New Zealand, 14 February 1930
BOURDA, Georgetown, Guyana, 21 February 1930
SABINA PARK, Kingston, Jamaica, 3 April 1930
THE GABBA, Brisbane, Australia, 27 November 1931
GYMKHANA GROUND, Bombay, India, 15 December 1933
EDEN GARDENS, Calcutta, India, 5 January 1934
CHEPAUK, Madras, India, 10 February 1934
KOTLA, New Delhi, India, 10 November 1948
BRABOURNE STADIUM, Bombay, Insia, 9 December 1948
ELLIS PARK, Johannesburg, South Africa, 27 December 1948
GREEN PARK STADIUM, Kanpur, India, 12 January 1952
UNIVERSITY GROUND, Lucknow, India, 23 October 1952
BANGABANDHU NATIONAL STADIUM, Dhaka, Pakistan,
1 January 1955
BAHAWAL STADIUM, Bahawalpur, Pakistan, 15 January 1955
BAGH-E-JINNAH, Lahore, Pakistan, 29 January 1955
ARBAB NIAZ STADIUM, Peshawar, Pakistan, 13 February 1955
NATIONAL STADIUM, Karachi, Pakistan, 26 February 1955
CARISBROOK, Dunedin, New Zealand, 11 March 1955
LAL BAHADUR SHASTRI STADIUM, Hyderabad, India,
19 November 1955
NEHRU STADIUM, Madras, India, 6 January 1956
WANDERERS, Johannesburg, South Africa, 24 December 1956
GADDAFI STADIUM, Lahore, Pakistan, 21 November 1959
PINDI CLUB GROUND, Rawalpindi, Pakistan, 27 March 1965
VCA GROUND, Nagpur, India, 3 October 1969
THE WACA, Perth, Australia, 11 December 1970
NIAZ STADIUM, Hyderabad, Pakistan, 16 March 1973
CHINNASWAMY STADIUM, Bangalore, India, 22 November 1974

WANKHEDE STADIUM, Bombay, India, 23 January 1975
IQBAL STADIUM, Faisalabad, Pakistan, 16 October 1978
McLEAN PARK, Napier, New Zealand, 16 February 1979
IBN-E-QASIM BAGH STADIUM, Multan, Pakistan,
30 December 1980
ANTIGUA RECREATION GROUND, St John's, Antigua,
27 March 1981
SARAVANAMUTTU STADIUM, Colombo, Sri Lanka, 17 February 1982
ASGIRIYA STADIUM, Kandy, Sri Lanka, 22 April 1983
GANDHI STADIUM, Jalandhar, India, 24 September 1983
SARDAR PATEL STADIUM, Ahmedabad, India, 12 November 1983
SINHALESE SPORTS CLUB GROUND, Colombo, Sri Lanka,
16 March 1984
COLOMBO CRICKET CLUB GROUND, Colombo, Sri Lanka,
24 March 1984
JINNAH STADIUM, Sialkot, Pakistan, 27 October 1985
BARABATI STADIUM, Cuttack, India, 4 January 1987
SAWAI MANSINGH STADIUM, Jaipur, India, 21 February 1987
BELLERIVE OVAL, Hobart, Tasmania, Australia, 16 December 1989
SECTOR 16 STADIUM, Chandigarh, India, 23 November 1990
WESTPAC PARK, Hamilton, New Zealand, 22 February 1991
JINNAH STADIUM, Gujranwala, Pakistan, 20 December 1991
PREMADASA STADIUM, Colombo, Sri Lanka, 28 August 1992
FERNANDO STADIUM, Moratuwa, Sri Lanka, 8 September 1992
HARARE SPORTS CLUB, Harare, Zimbabwe, 18 October 1992
BULAWAYO ATHLETIC CLUB, Bulawayo, Zimbabwe,
1 November 1992
DEFENCE CRICKET STADIUM, Karachi, Pakistan,
1 December 1993
RAWALPINDI CRICKET STADIUM, Rawalpindi, Pakistan,
9 December 1993
K.D. SINGH BABU STADIUM, Lucknow, India, 18 January 1994
QUEENS SPORTS CLUB, Bulawayo, Zimbabwe, 20 October 1994
PCA STADIUM, Mohali, India, 10 December 1994

PESHAWAR CLUB GROUND, Peshawar, Pakistan, 8 September 1995
SUPERSPORT PARK, Centurion, South Africa, 16 November 1995
SHEIKHUPURA STADIUM, Sheikhupura, Pakistan, 17 October 1996
ARNOS VALE GROUND, Kingstown, Saint Vincent, 20 June 1997
GALLE INTERNATIONAL STADIUM, Galle, Sri Lanka, 3 June 1998
GOODYEAR PARK, Bloemfontein, South Africa, 29 October 1999
MULTAN CRICKET STADIUM, Multan, Pakistan, 29 August 2001
CHITTAGONG STADIUM, Chittagong, Bangladesh, 15 November 2001
SCA STADIUM, Sharjah, United Arab Emirates, 31 January 2002
QUEEN'S PARK, St George's, Grenada, 28 June 2002
BUFFALO PARK, East London, South Africa, 18 October 2002
NORTH WEST CRICKET STADIUM, Potchefstroom, South Africa,
25 October 2002
RIVERSIDE GROUND, Chester-le-Street, England, 5 June 2003
BEAUSEJOUR STADIUM, Gros Islet, Saint Lucia, 20 June 2003
MARRAR OVAL, Darwin, Australia, 18 July 2003
BUNDABERG RUM STADIUM, Cairns, Australia, 25 July 2003

GROUNDS FOR CONCERN

WHEN CRICKET IS PLAYED on the Australian-ruled Lord Howe Island in the Pacific (population *c*.150), the ground is so small that only one end of the concrete pitch is covered with matting. At the end of each over, the fieldsmen stay put and the batsmen change over!

During the bitter English winter of 1879, a number of games were played on ice. On 9 January it was announced that a game of cricket would be 'played by Moonlight on the Ice in Windsor Home Park' at seven o'clock that evening. Several hundred spectators assembled, 'the game causing no end of amusement owing to the difficulties encountered by the players while bowling, batting, and fielding'.

An early ground of Rio de Janeiro Cricket Club was in the Rua Paysandu at the foot of a stone quarry.

Perched on a steep hill, the Ilfracombe Rugby Club ground at Hele presents an unusual challenge for fielders, as Paul Crabb discovered when playing for the Devon club's cricket section against Woolacombe in July 1996. When a ball was hit out of the ground, Crabb gave chase as it ran down a steep hill, finally catching up with it a quarter of a mile from the wicket. Just as he was about to tackle the long ascent, a bus came along. So he hopped on and caught the bus back to the ground, the driver even waiving the 46p fare.

Arguably the strangest cricket pitch in the world is on a sandbar in the middle of the Solent, the stretch of water between Hampshire and the Isle of Wight. Bramble Bank surfaces only twice a year for about an hour at a time when the water level is at its lowest at the spring and autumn equinox. The result is a sandbank measuring some two acres, liberally dotted with pools of water. Players arrive in a flotilla of boats and wear Wellington boots with their whites. A six is considered a lost ball. But there are fears that the annual match between the Royal Southern Yacht Club and the Island Sailing Club may soon have to be scrapped because of global warming, which could leave the pitch permanently waterlogged.

During the nineteenth century, intrepid British sailors laid down boat sails on the edge of the Sahara Desert to form a makeshift cricket square amid the sand dunes.

The world's most southerly game of cricket took place in Antarctica 700 km from the South Pole on 11 January 1985. The snow pitch was rolled by a Hercules transport aircraft, stumps were improvised, and the midnight sun allowed play to continue until 11 p.m. The two teams were made up of international scientists and environmentalists attending a conference at Beardmore South Camp. For the record the Gondwanaland Occasionals (Australians, New Zealanders and South Africans) beat the Beardmore Casuals (a mainly British team) by 27 runs.

In the late 1990s, High Farndale CC in North Yorkshire boasted an outfield that was an uncut meadow used by a local farmer to graze his herd of cattle. While the wicket itself was perfectly manicured, mid-on was buried under two feet of grass, rabbit burrows, badger setts and cow pats. One player admitted: 'Most teams like to play us early in the season when the grass is shorter. And when a chap fell down a badger hole, we brought the boundary in.'

BOWLERS WHO HAVE TAKEN MOST TEST WICKETS LBW

SHANE WARNE (Australia)	127
WASIM AKRAM (Pakistan)	119
ANIL KUMBLE (India)	118
KAPIL DEV (India)	110
WAQAR YOUNIS (Pakistan)	110
GLENN MCGRATH (Australia)	107
MUTTIAH MURALITHARAN (Sri Lanka)	99
RICHARD HADLEE (New Zealand)	83
IAN BOTHAM (England)	81
CHAMINDA VAAS (Sri Lanka)	81

SNOW JOKE

WITH ENGLAND STRUGGLING to make inroads against the West Indies at Trent Bridge in 1976, fast bowler John Snow decided to try to slow the game down to destroy the rhythm of the Windies' batsmen. So after lunch he went out with his pockets full of breadcrumbs, which he proceeded to scatter all over the ground. Within a matter of seconds, hundreds of pigeons descended, bringing play to a temporary halt. The match was eventually drawn.

When in the middle of a good innings my batting partner hit an early catch towards me, the desire for laughs overcame all other instincts. I dropped my bat and caught the ball. Such a bold defiance of the sport had its desired effect on the umpire. He ordered me off the field. Later, I was called to his room for six of the best. I didn't mind. I had won the round.

Actor JOHN LE MESURIER *on his schooldays,* A Jobbing Actor

STATISTICALLY SPEAKING

ONLY TWO BATSMEN have made a duck in the first innings of their Test debut and then scored a century in the second innings. India's Gundappa Viswanath made 0 and 137 against Australia at Kanpur in 1969–70, and Pakistan's Mohammad Wasim made 0 and 109 not out against New Zealand at Lahore, 1996–7.

Australia's Steve Waugh was involved in no fewer than twenty-seven run-outs in Test cricket, of which his partner was run out on twenty-three occasions. This means that in 85.2 per cent of the run-outs, it was Waugh's partner who paid the price. In the all-time list of partners to avoid, this puts Waugh second only to West Indies' Shivnarine Chanderpaul, who has been run out himself just twice in fourteen incidents – a record of 85.7 per cent.

When M. L. Jaisimha of India played against Australia at Calcutta in 1959–60, he became the first person to bat on all five days of a Test. Going in at number nine, he was 2 not out at the end of the first day and took his score to 20 not out on the next morning. On the third day he again went in late – this time at number four – and hadn't scored by the close of play. He then batted throughout the fourth day, scoring only 59 runs, before continuing on the fifth morning until finally being dismissed for 74.

In November 2002, seventeen-year-old A. T. Rayudu made 210 and 159 not out for Indian team Hyderabad against Andhra in what was only his third first-class match. In doing so, he became the youngest player ever to score a double-century and a century in the same first-class match, beating Don Bradman's 21 years 104 days.

There were 17 wides in the Japanese women's team's total of 28 against Pakistan in July 2003 – over 60 per cent of the score. Two days later Japan showed they could be similarly wayward by bowling a record-equalling 67 wides against Holland.

Of all the ways in which batsmen have been dismissed in Test cricket, the most frequent involving a combination of bowler and fielder is c Marsh b Lillee, which occurred 95 times.

In the 1956 Ashes series, England opening batsman Peter Richardson was caught at the wicket in every one of his eight dismissals.

The third-wicket partnership of 168 between Kumar Sangakkara and Mahela Jayawardene for Sri Lanka against South Africa at Durban in 2000–1 made up 77.78 per cent of the side's total of 216 – the highest percentage in Test cricket.

England's Freddie Brown won only three out of fifteen tosses, making him the world's unluckiest Test captain with the coin, along with New Zealand's Glenn Turner, who won just two from ten.

When Surrey pace bowler Jimmy Ormond dismissed Middlesex batsmen Ben Hutton, Ed Joyce and Paul Weekes with successive balls in 2003, it was the first recorded hat-trick composed purely of left-handers in British first-class cricket. Earlier in the same over Ormond had claimed the wicket of another left-hander, Andrew Strauss.

Aged thirty-six, Shane Warne broke Dennis Lillee's record of 85 Test wickets in a year by taking 96 Test wickets in 2005.

THE TEA INTERVAL

BEFORE THE INTRODUCTION of the tea interval, players would take it in turns to leave the field for a few minutes, thus leaving the fielding side a man short, either for a cup of tea or perhaps some-

thing stronger. Now the twenty-minute tea interval is an accepted part of the day's schedule – an opportunity for players and umpires alike to take a comfort break and a spot of light refreshment – and as such is governed by Law 15, the sections of which include:

Changing agreed times for intervals.
If for adverse conditions of ground, weather or light, or for any other reason, playing time is lost, the umpires and captains together may alter the time of the lunch interval or of the tea interval.

Changing agreed time for tea interval.
[a] (i) If an innings ends when thirty minutes or less remain before the agreed time for tea, then the interval shall be taken immediately. It shall be of the agreed length and shall be considered to include the ten minutes between innings.

   (ii) If, when thirty minutes remain before the agreed time for tea, an interval between innings is already in progress, play will resume at the end of the ten-minute interval.

[b] (i) If, because of adverse conditions of ground, weather or light, or in exceptional circumstances, a stoppage occurs when thirty minutes or less remain before the agreed time for tea, then unless either there is an agreement to change the time for tea, as permitted in 5 above or the captains agree to forgo the tea interval, as permitted in 10 below, the interval shall be taken immediately. The interval shall be of the agreed

length. Play shall resume at the end of this interval or as soon after as conditions permit.

(ii) If a stoppage is already in progress when thirty minutes remain before the time agreed for tea, 5 above will apply.

8. *Tea interval – nine wickets down.*

If nine wickets are down at the end of the over in progress when the agreed time for the tea interval has been reached, then play shall continue for a period not exceeding thirty minutes, unless the players have cause to leave the field of play, or the innings is concluded earlier.

10. *Agreement to forgo intervals.*

At any time during the match, the captains may agree to forgo the tea interval or any of the drinks intervals. The umpires shall be informed of the decision.

BATSMEN WHO WERE OUT
IN THE 90S ON THEIR TEST DEBUT

HON. STANLEY JACKSON – 91 (England v Australia, Lord's, 1893)

LOUIS TANCRED – 97 (South Africa v Australia, Johannesburg, 1902–3)

ROY MINNETT – 90 (Australia v England, Sydney, 1911–12)

ARTHUR RICHARDSON – 98 (Australia v England, Sydney, 1924–5)

ARTHUR CHIPPERFIELD – 99 (Australia v England, Trent Bridge, 1934)

PAUL GIBB – 93 (England v South Africa, Johannesburg, 1938–9)

VICTOR STOLLMEYER – 96 (West Indies v England, Oval, 1939)

ROBERT CHRISTIANI – 99 (West Indies v England, Bridgetown, 1947–8)

FRANK WORRELL – 97 (West Indies v England, Port of Spain, 1947–8)

PERCY MANSELL – 90 (South Africa v England, Headingley, 1951)

JOHN HOLT – 94 (West Indies v England, Kingston, 1953–4)

NOEL HARFORD – 93 (New Zealand v Pakistan, Lahore, 1955–6)

IAN REDPATH – 97 (Australia v South Africa, Melbourne, 1963–4)

ABDUL KADIR – 95 (Pakistan v Australia, Karachi, 1964–5)

COLIN MILBURN – 94 (England v West Indies, Old Trafford, 1966)

BARRY WOOD – 90 (England v Australia, Oval, 1972)

GORDON GREENIDGE – 93 (West Indies v India, Bangalore, 1974–5)

ROBERT ANDERSON – 92 (New Zealand v Pakistan, Lahore, 1976–7)

BRUCE LAIRD – 92 (Australia v West Indies, Brisbane, 1979–80)

TASLIM ARIF – 90 (Pakistan v India, Calcutta, 1979–80)

JACK RUSSELL – 94 (England v Sri Lanka, Lord's, 1988)

STEPHEN FLEMING – 92 (New Zealand v India, Hamilton, 1993–4)

CHAMARA DUNUSINGHE – 91 (Sri Lanka v New Zealand, Napier, 1994–5)

RICKY PONTING – 96 (Australia v Sri Lanka, Perth, 1995–6)

RAHUL DRAVID – 95 (India v England, Lord's, 1996)

ASIM KAMAL – 99 (Pakistan v South Africa, Lahore, 2003–4)

IS THERE A DOCTOR IN THE HOUSE?

IN TRYING TO SAVE a boundary against Lancashire at Old Trafford in July 1887, Gloucestershire's Arthur Croome ran into the railings in front of the pavilion and fell on the spikes, which made a deep wound in his throat. Fortunately, Dr W. G. Grace was in the Gloucestershire team that day and was able to save his teammate's life. Croome later wrote in admiration: 'They had to send out for a needle and thread to sew it up, and for nearly half an hour W. G. held the edges of the wound together. It was of vital importance that the injured part should be kept absolutely still and his hand never shook all that time ... It would have been a remarkable feat of endurance under any circumstances, but the Old Man had been fielding out for over four hundred runs and had done his share of bowling, evidence of W. G.'s amazing stamina.'

FROM *Jerks In From Short Leg*
BY R. A. FITZGERALD (1866)

THE PLODDING CRICKETER. To our mind this type is the most painful and most mysterious of all. He plays in more matches than all the other types collected. His name is always found in the penultimate order of going in. He is very seldom a bowler, and is at best a long stop. Yet he hammers on, like the fabulous horse, on the 'ard 'ard road to honour and glory. He is the best-tempered fellow in the world, and his name appears weekly in some facetious contribution to the sporting prints, under some new nom de guerre. You may catch him any afternoon at practice; and when he isn't oiling his bat, he is reading *Lillywhite's Guide and Advice to Cricketers*.

Now, in what lies the secret of his attachment to the game? Can it be a thirst for success? Surely such a prospect can be but a mirage. Cricket has much of the will-o'-the-wisp delusion about it; it holds out to the plodding cricketer a sufficient glimmer of momentary success to light him on his path; it has so many funny turns and slices of luck, that the most erratic must sometimes fall into the right groove, and the most hungry come in for an unexpected innings at its board.

The Plodder is after all a very useful man in the field. He will always field out when you are a man 'short' (and when you are not?) and will, if properly appealed to, for the sake of cricket, go so far as to carry your bag to the railway station; and we hope cricket will never be without many representatives of this little appreciated but valuable type.

FIERY FRED

YORKSHIRE WERE PLAYING OXBRIDGE and following the fall of a University wicket a slim figure, elegantly attired in spotless Savile Row flannels and new boots, came out to bat. He wore his cap at a jaunty angle and had a silk scarf around his neck. On his way to the crease he demonstrated perfectly timed strokes which despatched the imaginary bowlers to all parts of the ground. The Yorkshire players watched his approach in silence. Surveying the scene imperiously, he then took guard and spent a whole minute making his block hole. Finally, after another study of the field placings, he was ready to receive his first ball. Freddie Trueman bowled it and knocked two of the stumps clean out of the ground. As the batsman turned and walked languidly back to the pavilion, Trueman called out: 'Bad luck, sir. You were just getting settled in.'

Dr W. G. Grace
Had hair all over his face.
Lord! how the people cheered
When a ball got lost in his beard!

E. C. BENTLEY

BAD DAY AT THE OFFICE

- The last man in for Glamorgan against the Indian tourists at Cardiff, Peter Judge was bowled first ball by Sarwate. To save time when Glamorgan followed on, Judge kept his pads on and opened the batting. Once again, he was clean-bowled by Sarwate first ball, for the quickest 'pair' in history.

- Playing for Kent against Sussex at Brighton in 1891, Mr C. J. M. Fox was not out at lunch in the second innings, but left the ground to dine with friends and returned too late to resume his knock. In his absence Kent were skittled for 54.

- In fourteen consecutive innings in 1907, Yorkshire's George Deyes had scores of 0, 0, 0 not out, 1, 1 not out, 0, 0, 0, 0, 1 not out, 0, 0, 0, 0.

- Fielding at gully for Gentlemen v Players at Scarborough in 1920, Greville Stevens dropped Wilfred Rhodes off three successive balls in one over.

- Young Surrey batsman Frederick Buckle failed to distinguish himself against Middlesex in 1869. In the first innings he was recorded as 'Absent, not sent for in time – 0' and in the second as 'Absent unwell – 0.'

- Derbyshire bowler John Kelly ended up with the unfortunate figures of 0–0–4–0 against Lancashire at Old Trafford in July 1955. His first and only delivery was a no-ball, hit for four by Jack Dyson.

- The most expensive first over in first-class cricket was bowled by Oxford University leg-spinner Stephen Moreton to Gloucestershire's New Zealand Test batsman Craig Spearman at The Parks in April 2005. Moreton was hit for 6, 6, 6, 6, 4 and 6 – a total of 34 runs.

- Bowling in a Queensland country match during the 1968–9 season, R. Grubb conceded 62 runs off one eight-ball over. The batsman struck nine sixes and two fours off the over, which also included four no-balls.

- Chris Purdie of Tilford dropped Gary Cox off the first ball of his over in a 1998 match against Redingensians in Surrey and went on to concede 40 from the over. The dropped catch went for four and Cox hit the next six balls for six. This included a no-ball after Purdie switched to bowling round the wicket without first informing the umpire.

- In 1960, actor Trevor Howard agreed to appear in a charity match at Buxton. To do so, he got up at 5 a.m., journeyed 180 miles to Derbyshire and was caught behind first ball.

- On his first-class debut for Lancashire against Hampshire in August 1995, Andrew Flintoff scored 7 and 0, and also dropped five catches.

- In 1920, Dr Roy Park made a solitary Test appearance for Australia against England at Melbourne. He was out first ball in his only innings and bowled just one over, which yielded nine runs. It is said that Park's wife, who was sitting in the stands, dropped her knitting at the crucial moment and so missed his innings.

- In 1990, Northamptonshire tail-ender Mark Robinson went twelve first-class innings from 4 May until 15 September without scoring a single run. Another Northants bowler, Jim Griffiths, made ten successive noughts (including not-out innings) in the mid-1970s.

- In 1989, Twyford CC near Bristol staged a match to raise funds for urgently needed ground maintenance. It raised £44, but in the course of the match a window was broken by a six and the club had to spend £45 on repairs.

- After being 1 not out overnight against Surrey at the Oval in 1921, Leicestershire wicketkeeper Thomas Sidwell was unable to resume his innings the following morning because he got lost on the London Underground. He was recorded in the scorebook as 'absent, lost on Tube'.

- Yorkshire and England bowler Ryan Sidebottom ended the National League match with Glamorgan at Headingley in 2003 with figures of 0.1–0–11–0. He bowled two wides, one short ball (hooked for six), and three more leg-side wides before retiring with a tight hamstring.

- The most expensive dropped catch was made by Durham wicketkeeper Chris Scott, who put down Brian Lara when the West Indian batsman had made just 18 for Warwickshire at Edgbaston in 1994. Lara, who had earlier been bowled by a no-ball, was in prime form at the time, leading Scott to lament: 'I suppose he'll get a hundred now.' Lara went on to make 501 not out – the highest innings in first-class history.

The Fastest Deliveries of the World's Fastest Bowlers

		mph
1.	Shoaib Akhtar (Pakistan)	100.23
2.	Brett Lee (Australia)	99.9
3.	Mohammad Sami (Pakistan)	97.2
4.	Nantie Hayward (South Africa)	95.9
5.	Jason Gillespie (Australia)	95.6
6.	Steve Harmison (England)	95.0
7.	Shane Bond (New Zealand)	94.3
8.	Andrew Flintoff (England)	94.3
9.	Fidel Edwards (West Indies)	93.0
10.	Makhaya Ntini (South Africa)	92.8

FIVE FAMOUS RUN-INS WITH UMPIRES

Rohan Kanhai and Arthur Fagg, Edgbaston, 1973

WHEN ENGLISH UMPIRE Arthur Fagg rejected an appeal against Geoff Boycott for a catch behind off Keith Boyce, West Indian captain Rohan Kanhai reacted angrily, all the more so as Boycott went on to share a first-wicket stand of 96 with Dennis Amiss. Fagg was so incensed by the player's ungentlemanly response that he announced he was going home in the middle of the Test. True to his word, Fagg refused to take his position on the third morning and was temporarily replaced by Warwickshire coach Alan Oakman. However, Fagg soon relented and went on to resume his duties.

Dennis Lillee and John King, Col Timmins, Brisbane, 1984

LESS THAN FOUR WEEKS AFTER making his final appearance for Australia, Dennis Lillee was captaining Western Australia in a Sheffield Shield match against Queensland when he became involved in a row with umpires John King and Col Timmins over a drinks break. Although the umpires had decreed that drinks should not be taken because the morning session had been shortened by rain, Lillee appeared to overrule them by ordering drinks to be brought on to the field. The umpires reported Lillee for acting in a 'provocative and disapproving manner', and he was suspended from all cricket for a month despite pleading that he had simply misinterpreted the rules.

Mike Gatting and Shakoor Rana, Faisalabad, 1987

AFTER PAKISTAN UMPIRE Shakoor Rana accused England captain Mike Gatting of cheating in the second Test, by moving a fielder behind the batsman's back while Eddie Hemmings was bowling,

Gatting and Rana became involved in an eyeball-to-eyeball, finger jabbing confrontation in the middle of the pitch. Rana refused to stand again in the match until Gatting apologized. Even though he had been wrongly accused in the first place, Gatting offered an apology and the match continued, but only after the third day had been abandoned because Pakistan elected to remain in the pavilion in support of Rana. The incident led to such ill-feeling between the two nations that England didn't tour Pakistan again for another thirteen years.

Phil Tufnell and Peter O'Connell, Melbourne, 1990

WHEN ENGLAND'S PHIL TUFNELL innocently asked, 'How many left, ump?', Australian umpire Peter O'Connell replied, 'Count them yourself, you Pommy bastard!' That O'Connell is said to have 'looked Tufnell up and down with barely disguised distaste' before answering merely served to confirm his status as a living legend Down Under.

Arjuna Ranatunga and Darrell Hair, Melbourne, 1995

SRI LANKAN CAPTAIN Arjuna Ranatunga angrily confronted Australian umpire Darrell Hair after the latter had called his star bowler, Muttiah Muralitharan, for throwing. Ranatunga left the field, but when he returned he put Muralitharan on from the other end, where New Zealand umpire Steve Dunne was standing. Although Dunne didn't call Muralitharan, the controversy over the bowler's action still rages ten years on.

NON-WICKETKEEPERS WITH THE MOST TEST CATCHES

MARK WAUGH (Australia)	181
MARK TAYLOR (Australia)	157
ALLAN BORDER (Australia)	156
BRIAN LARA (West Indies)	148
STEPHEN FLEMING (New Zealand)	140
RAHUL DRAVID (India)	129
GREG CHAPPELL (Australia)	122
VIV RICHARDS (West Indies)	122
IAN BOTHAM (England)	120
COLIN COWDREY (England)	120
SHANE WARNE (Australia)	118
CARL HOOPER (West Indies)	115
RICKY PONTING (Australia)	115
STEVE WAUGH (Australia)	112
WALLY HAMMOND (England)	110
BOBBY SIMPSON (Australia)	110
GARY SOBERS (West Indies)	109
SUNIL GAVASKAR (India)	108
MOHAMMED AZHARUDDIN (India)	105
IAN CHAPPELL (Australia)	105

CRICKET AND POLITICS

- As LORD DUNGLASS, former British Prime Minister **Sir Alec Douglas-Home** played first-class cricket for Middlesex (1924–5) and went on the MCC tour to South America of 1926–7.

- **Francis H. D. Bell**, who played for Wellington (1873–7), became New Zealand Prime Minister for two weeks in 1925.

- **Lord Foster of Lepe** played for Oxford University and Hampshire (1885–95) before becoming MP for Sevenoaks and Governor-General of Australia (1920–5).

- **Hon. Alfred Lyttelton** played for Middlesex and in four Tests for England (1880–4). He was then made Britain's Colonial Secretary from 1903 to 1905.

- **The Duke of Wellington** played for All Ireland against The Garrison in 1792, scoring 5 and 1. He later became British Prime Minister.

- **Hon. Charles Lyttelton** captained Worcestershire from 1936 to 1939. Later, as Viscount Cobham, he served as Governor-General of New Zealand from 1957 to 1962.

- **Thomas Freeman** of Cambridge University and Sussex (1886–90) went on to become Lord Willingdon, Governor-General of Canada from 1926 to 1931.

- **Hon. Sir Francis Stanley Jackson** was a stylish middle-order batsman for Yorkshire and England (1893–1905) and was later appointed Governor of Bengal.

- **Sir Kynaston Studd**, a former Middlesex cricketer, was named Lord Mayor of London in 1928.
- **Hon. Frederic Thesiger** played for Oxford University and Middlesex before, as Viscount Chelmsford, becoming Viceroy of India from 1916 to 1921.

From the Commentary Box

Like an old lady poking with her umbrella at a wasp's nest.
JOHN ARLOTT *describing the batting*
of Australia's Ernie Toshack

He approaches the wicket like Groucho Marx
chasing a pretty waitress.
JOHN ARLOTT *on crouching run–up*
of Pakistan bowler Asif Masood

The umpire signals a bye with the air of a weary stork.
JOHN ARLOTT

Umpire Harold Bird, having a wonderful time,
signalling everything in the world, including stopping traffic
coming on from behind.
JOHN ARLOTT

He played a cut so late as to be positively posthumous.
JOHN ARLOTT

[Graham] Thorpe just nibbles that,
nurdles it down to third man.
HENRY BLOFELD

[Graeme] Hick scratches around like an old hen
in the crease there.
HENRY BLOFELD

The Queen's Park Oval, exactly as its name suggests –
absolutely round.
TONY COZIER

Laird has been brought in to stand in the corner of the circle.
RICHIE BENAUD

The first time you face up to a googly you're going to be in
trouble if you've never faced one before.
TREVOR BAILEY

Turner looks a bit shaky and unsteady,
but I think he's going to bat on – one ball left.
BRIAN JOHNSTON, *after New Zealand's Glenn Turner
was struck in the box area by the penultimate ball of the over*

Anyone foolish enough to predict the outcome
of this match is a fool.
FRED TRUEMAN

Yorkshire were 232 all out, Hutton ill.
No, I'm sorry, Hutton III.
JOHN SNAGGE

On the first day, Logie decided to chance his arm
and it came off.
TREVOR BAILEY

Fred Titmus has two short legs, one of them square.
BRIAN JOHNSTON

The bowler's Holding, the batsman's Willey.
BRIAN JOHNSTON *commentating on a 1976 Test
when England batsman Peter Willey faced
West Indies fast bowler Michael Holding*

You've come over to Leicester at a very appropriate time
where the captain Ray Illingworth has just relieved himself
at the pavilion end.
BRIAN JOHNSTON

EPITAPH TO AN ANONYMOUS CRICKETER

*As in life so in death lies a bat of renown,
Slain by a lorry (three ton);
His innings is over, his bat is laid down:
To the end a poor judge of a run.*

GEORGE McWILLIAM

THREE AMAZING TURNAROUNDS

AT THE ANNUAL Eton v Harrow match at Lord's in 1910, Harrow made 232 and then bowled Eton out for 67. Following on, Eton were just four runs ahead with one wicket standing before a courageous stand of 50 in under 25 minutes between the Hon. J. N. Manners (40 not out) and Mr K. Lister Kaye (13) took the total to 219, leaving Harrow 55 to win. Victory seemed a formality, but Harrow had reckoned without the deceptive off-breaks of Mr Robert St Leger Fowler, who took 8 for 23 to hustle them out for 45.

Hampshire pulled off a comprehensive victory over Warwickshire at Edgbaston in 1922 after being bowled out for 15 in their first innings. Batting first, Warwickshire made 223 before skittling the visitors for 15. Following on, Hampshire were struggling at 186–6, but centuries from George Brown (172) and Walter Livsey (110 not out) helped lift the total to 521. Warwickshire were then dismissed for 158, leaving Hampshire the winners by 155 runs.

Essex made 642 in their first innings against Glamorgan at Chelmsford in 2004, but still managed to lose the match. In reply Glamorgan were tottering at 286–7 before recovering to 587 all out. They then bowled Essex out for 165 and reached their target of 221 with four wickets to spare.

OVER AND OUT

THE EARLIEST RULES of cricket specified that four balls were bowled in each over. In 1889, four-ball overs were replaced by five-ball overs, which were then increased to six balls an over in 1900 – the figure that England has adopted ever since, apart from an experiment with the eight-ball over in 1939. Australia, New Zealand, South Africa and Pakistan have all utilized the eight-ball over at some stage, Australia and New Zealand only curtailing the practice as recently as the 1979–80 season. The 2000 code only permits six-ball overs.

LITERARY CONNECTIONS

- **SIR ARTHUR CONAN DOYLE** played cricket for the MCC. He hit a century on his debut, had bowling figures of 7 for 51 against Cambridgeshire at Lord's in 1899, and once bowled out W. G. Grace. Moreover, he took the name of Sherlock Holmes from the Derbyshire cricketer F. Shacklock. Another Derbyshire player, Thomas Mycroft, inspired the name of Holmes' brother, Mycroft.

- Playwright **TERENCE RATTIGAN** earned a place in the Harrow School XI of 1929 as an opening bat.

- An accomplished batsman and spin bowler, author
  C. P. Snow was captain of Newton's Grammar School,
  Leicester.

- Poet **Rupert Brooke** played for Rugby School in 1906,
  heading the school's bowling averages with 19 wickets at
  14.05 runs apiece.

- **Samuel Beckett** played for Dublin University against
  Northants in 1925 and 1926.

- As a schoolboy, **Lord Byron** scored 7 and 2 for Harrow
  against Eton in 1805.

- Joseph Wells, father of **H. G. Wells**, was a professional
  cricketer who took four wickets in four balls for Kent
  against Sussex in 1862. Among his quartet of victims was
  Spencer Austen-Leigh, the great-nephew of **Jane Austen**.

- **A. A. Milne** played for Westminster School in 1900 and
  1901.

- Poet **Siegfried Sassoon** played occasionally for
  Tunbridge Wells CC.

- **John Fowles**, author of *The French Lieutenant's Woman*,
  played for Bedford School (1942–4) and as a promising
  swing bowler had a trial for Essex.

- **P. G. Wodehouse** played for Dulwich College in 1899
  and 1900. In his second year he boasted a batting average of
  6.00 and took seven wickets for 114 runs. In 1913,
  Wodehouse saw Percy Jeeves, a promising medium-paced
  bowler, playing for Warwickshire and duly immortalized
  him by taking his name for his fictional butler. Jeeves the
  cricketer was killed during the First World War while
  serving with the Royal Warwickshire Regiment.

DICKENSIAN REFERENCES

CHARLES DICKENS was a keen follower of cricket and arranged a number of charity games where he would pay a guinea if the first ball (usually bowled by him) were hit to the boundary. References to cricket in his novels include:

Pickwick Papers (Chapter 7)
The Old Curiosity Shop (Chapter 15)
Bleak House (Chapter 4)
Martin Chuzzlewit (Chapters 4 and 5)
Great Expectations (Chapter 27)
Little Dorrit (Book II, Chapter 6)
The Mystery of Edwin Drood (Chapter 17)

The most celebrated of these is the cricket match between All-Muggleton and Dingley Dell in *Pickwick Papers*:

All-Muggleton had the first innings; and the interest became intense when Mr Dumkins and Mr Podder, two of the most renowned members of that most distinguished club, walked, bat in hand, to their respective wickets. Mr Luffey, the highest ornament of Dingley Dell, was pitched

to bowl against the redoubtable Dumkins, and Mr Struggles was selected
to do the same kind office for the hitherto unconquered Podder. Several
players were stationed, to 'look out', in different parts of the field, and
each fixed himself into the proper attitude by placing one hand on each
knee, and stooping very much as if he were 'making a back' for some
beginner at leap-frog. All the regular players do this sort of thing; –
indeed it is generally supposed that it is quite impossible to look out
properly in any other position.

The umpires were stationed behind the wickets; the scorers were
prepared to notch the runs; a breathless silence ensued. Mr Luffey retired
a few paces behind the wicket of the passive Podder, and applied the ball
to his right eye for several seconds. Dumkins confidently awaited its
coming with his eyes fixed on the motions of Luffey.

'Play!' suddenly cried the bowler. The ball flew from his hand straight
and swift towards the centre stump of the wicket. The wary Dumkins
was on the alert: it fell upon the tip of the bat, and bounded far away over
the heads of the scouts, who had just stooped low enough to let it fly over
them.

'Run–run—another.—Now, then throw her up—up with her—stop
there—another—no—yes—no—throw her up, throw her up!'—Such
were the shouts which followed the stroke; and at the conclusion of
which All-Muggleton had scored two. Nor was Podder behindhand in
earning laurels wherewith to garnish himself and Muggleton. He blocked
the doubtful balls, missed the bad ones, took the good ones, and sent
them flying to all parts of the field. The scouts were hot and tired; the
bowlers were changed and bowled till their arms ached; but Dumkins
and Podder remained unconquered. Did an elderly gentleman essay to
stop the progress of the ball, it rolled between his legs or slipped between
his fingers. Did a slim gentleman try to catch it, it struck him on the
nose, and bounded pleasantly off with redoubled violence, while the slim
gentleman's eyes filled with water, and his form writhed with anguish.
Was it thrown straight up to the wicket, Dumkins had reached it before
the ball. In short, when Dumkins was caught out, and Podder stumped
out, All-Muggleton had notched some fifty-four, while the score of the

Dingley Dellers was as blank as their faces. The advantage was too great to be recovered. In vain did the eager Luffey, and the enthusiastic Struggles, do all that skill and experience could suggest, to regain the ground Dingley Dell had lost in the contest – it was of no avail; and in an early period of the winning game Dingley Dell gave in, and allowed the superior prowess of All-Muggleton.

BARD FROM THE PAVILION?

EVEN THOUGH THE GAME was barely mentioned in his lifetime, some writers have endeavoured to identify references to cricket in Shakespeare's works, most notably:

> 'What work's, my countrymen, in hand? Where go you
> With bats and clubs?'
> *Coriolanus*

> 'Take my cap – Jupiter!'
> *Coriolanus*

'I had rather be set quick i' the earth
And bowl'd to death with turnips!'
The Merry Wives of Windsor, Act III, Scene IV

'And have is have, however men do catch.'
King John, Act I, Scene I

'Such wanton, wild, and usual slips
As are companions noted and most known.'
Hamlet, Act II, Scene I

'Yet would I knew that stroke would prove the worst!'
Othello, Act IV, Scene I

'We may outrun,
By violent swiftness, that which we run at,
And lose by over-running.'
Henry VIII, Act I, Scene I

'O, let the hours be short
Till fields, and blows, and groans applaud our sport.'
Henry IV, Part One, Act I, Scene III

'Gower is a goot captain, and is goot knowledge
and literatured in the wars.'
Henry V, Act IV, Scene VII

JACK WAS NO ACE

ONE OF THE BRIEFEST and least distinguished Ashes careers
belonged to New South Wales opening batsman Jack Moroney,
who was chosen to play in the First Test against England at
Brisbane in the 1950–1 series. In the first innings he lasted four balls

until he was caught at leg slip by Len Hutton off Trevor Bailey, but in the second innings he fared even worse, surviving just three deliveries before being trapped lbw to Bailey. Moroney was dropped for the next Test and was never again selected to face England. Thus his entire Ashes career lasted seven balls and provided him with a pair.

BLANK DAY

A TEAM OF BLANKS played against Staffordshire club Cannock Wood in 1998 after club member Alan Blank put together an eleven composed entirely of his relatives to fill in a blank day in the Cannock Wood fixture list. Another Blank umpired.

Wicketkeepers: Highest Innings Totals in Tests Without a Bye

713–3 dec Tatenda Taibu (Zimbabwe v Sri Lanka, Bulawayo, 2004)
671–4 Hashan Tillakaratne (Sri Lanka v New Zealand, Wellington, 1990–1)
660–5 dec Adam Parore (New Zealand v West Indies, Wellington, 1994–5)
659–8 dec Godfrey Evans (England v Australia, Sydney, 1946–7)
658–9 dec Ridley Jacobs (West Indies v South Africa, Durban, 2003–4)
652 Syed Kirmani (India v Pakistan, Faisalabad, 1982–3)
632–4 dec Alec Stewart (England v Australia, Lord's, 1993)
619 Jackie Hendriks (West Indies v Australia, Sydney, 1968–9)
616–5 dec Ian Smith (New Zealand v Pakistan, Auckland, 1988–9)
610–6 dec Sameer Dighe (India v Sri Lanka, Colombo, 2001)

'Pome' on Himself

A bowler there was name of Parkin
Who had too much liking for larkin';
He made people stare
And provoked a 'Lord's' prayer,
And he set all the little dogs barkin'.

Cecil Parkin

(A cunning slow bowler, Parkin was one of the mainstays of the Lancashire attack after the First World War. He was an incorrigible clown who would sing loudly as he came into bowl and would sometimes swap the ball for an orange. Once, with an orange concealed in the palm of his hand, he pretended to make an impossible pick-up and splattered the fruit into the gloves of wicketkeeper George Duckworth.)

An Unusual Injury XI

Nigel Briers. Fielding against Lancashire in 1993, the Leicestershire captain succeeded in spraining his thumb when he caught it in his trouser pocket.

Mark Butcher. In 2004 the England batsman strained a thigh muscle while tidying up some boxes at home.

Ted Dexter. The former England captain broke a leg when he was run over by his own Jaguar in 1965.

Chris Lewis. On the 1993–4 tour to the West Indies, the England all-rounder decided to go for a new image and shaved his head. In the opening match, he left his hat off and suffered sunstroke.

Ian Greig. Returning home from playing for Sussex in the early 1980s, Greig snapped his key in the lock. He tried to rectify the situation by breaking into his house, but broke an ankle instead when he fell off the side of the building. Then, in 1987, he went to hospital for a check-up on a broken finger sustained while batting against Pakistan, but ended up having his head stitched after walking into the X-ray machine.

Jon Fellows-Smith. Captaining Northants on a wet wicket in the early 1960s, the South African chose to lead by example when his pace men seemed reluctant to open the bowling. Assuring them that there was nothing treacherous about the surface, he promptly slipped on his run-up, broke his ankle and was stretchered off to hospital.

Derek Pringle. In 1982 the England all-rounder had to miss a Test match after injuring his back while writing a letter.

Mark Boucher. Touring Australia in 2000, the South African wicketkeeper sliced through his own hand while enjoying a snack in his hotel room.

Chris Old. The former Yorkshire and England bowler missed one game when he sneezed violently and damaged a rib.

Don Topley. Pushing a note through a friend's door, the Essex player got his hand trapped in the letterbox and had to miss the 1989 pre-season matches.

Terry Alderman. The Australian seamer was sidelined for a year with a dislocated shoulder after rugby-tackling an England fan who had invaded the pitch at Perth during the 1982–3 tour.

CLEAN HIT

SUSSEX BOWLER JOHN SNOW decided to liven up a dull clash with Leicestershire in the 1960s by bowling a ball made entirely of red soap. Batsman Peter Marner's flashing blade duly smashed it to pieces, whereupon both teams collapsed with laughter. The scorebook recorded the incident with the words: 'Ball exploded.'

FROM *The Field*, JULY 1922

A correspondent writes: 'The following incident, which I saw when playing at Hurstborne Park, may be worth recording, as it is not likely to happen again. The batsman ran for a bye, short slip gathered the ball and threw at the wicket, hitting the top of the centre stump. That batsman was given in, but the ball rose high from the top of the centre stump, went over the other running batsman, and pitched on the other wicket, and he was run out.'

A BREAKDOWN OF W. G. GRACE'S
126 FIRST-CLASS HUNDREDS (1866–1904)

51 for Gloucestershire
15 for Gentlemen (v Players)
15 for MCC and Ground
10 for the South
7 for London County
7 for Gentlemen of the South
6 for Gentlemen of England
5 for England
4 for MCC
2 for South of Thames
1 for Gloucestershire and Kent
1 for Gloucestershire and Yorkshire
1 for United South
1 for Single (v Married)

SCORE BOOK

The Score book gives the outline of the match,
Who scored the runs, who bowled with due success,
But only mentions Jones's lyric catch
And Thompson's epic stand, with casualness.
Caught Jones, bowled Smith, so runs the level prose
Of Jones's running catch far in the deep.
Thompson, bowled Johnson, nought, the legend goes,
As though he made one ineffective sweep.
He was the last man in, and long he stayed,
And all the bowlers' onslaughts he defied.
He kept his end up while his partner made
The runs that won the victory for his side.
The book omits the poetry of Cricket,
How Brown superbly bowled, but took no wicket.

W. A. G. KEMP

RUNNING SCARED

DENIS COMPTON was infamous for his running between wickets,
leading to the demise of many an innocent partner. Trevor Bailey
remembered batting with him at the 1954 Old Trafford Test against

Pakistan. 'I set off for a run when Denis called me, and I was a third of the way down the pitch when he yelled, "Wait!" Then he said, "no" as we passed each other. So you might say I was a victim of the three-call trick.'

TEST CRICKETERS IN THE ARTS

- IAN BOTHAM (England) made his theatrical debut as The King in a 1991 production of *Jack and the Beanstalk*.

- MERV HUGHES (Australia) has made a guest appearance in the Channel 9 drama *Flying Doctors*.

- JACK RUSSELL (England) is a talented artist whose paintings change hands for up to £25,000 each.

- MAX WALKER (Australia) was named his country's best-selling author in 1990 after three of his books – *How to Hypnotize Chooks*, *How to Tame Lions* and *How to Kiss a Crocodile* – each sold over 150,000 copies.

- RICHARD ELLISON (England) appeared in the Canterbury Opera Society version of *Fiddler on the Roof* in 1985.

- DARREN GOUGH (England) appeared in *The Beano* comic in 2003, in a cartoon featuring the character Billy Whizz, and in 2005 he won the BBC celebrity TV show *Strictly Come Dancing*.

- DEREK PRINGLE (England) made a brief appearance in the 1981 film *Chariots of Fire*.

- SHANE WARNE (Australia) and Graham Gooch (England) have promoted hair-replacement treatment in a TV commercial filmed at the Oval.

- PHIL TUFNELL (England) won the reality TV series *I'm A Celebrity, Get Me Out Of Here!* in 2003.

- BEV CONGDON (New Zealand) played trumpet in a jazz band.

- JOHN SNOW (England) had two volumes of his poetry published in the 1970s.

- RICKY PONTING (Australia) once dressed up as a deodorant can for an advertisement.

- TONY LEWIS (England) was a violinist with the Welsh Youth Orchestra.

DEDICATED FOLLOWERS OF FASHION

EIGHTEENTH-CENTURY CRICKETERS wore three-cornered or jockey hats, often with silver or gold lace, frilled shirts, white flannel breeches, silk stockings and buckled shoes. From about 1810 trousers started to replace breeches, and players wore tall hats in black or white. Shirts were no longer frilled but came with high collars and

bow ties, professionals often distinguishing themselves by wearing braces. By the mid-nineteenth century the tall hat had been replaced by a soft white cap or a straw hat, and short white flannel jackets had become popular. Between 1850 and 1880 club cricket colours began to appear (the first MCC uniform was in azure blue), often as ribbons worn around bowler hats. Players of this era wore striped or spotted shirts, boots replaced shoes, and blazers were introduced. To guard against the traditional English summer, the sweater also made its bow towards the end of the century.

The MCC touring cap and blazer were first worn by the team that visited Australia in 1903–4 under the captaincy of Pelham Warner. A cap awarded to England players in Test matches at home was introduced in 1908. A touring cap bearing the arms of Australia was first worn by the team that visited England in 1890.

In the days of underarm and round-arm bowling, umpires wore black suits, but when overarm bowling arrived on the scene, batsmen complained that they could not see the ball against the background of the umpire's dark suit. So in 1861 white overcoats became the umpire's designated mode of attire.

To protect his legs, the noted Surrey batsman Robert Robinson had, around 1800, taken the field wearing a pair of home-made wooden pads – two thin boards set at an angle to guard his shin. But they made such a noise when in contact with the ball that he was subjected to ridicule and soon abandoned them. Modern-style pads were first worn in the Sussex v England match at Brighton in 1839. Special gloves for wicketkeepers were introduced in 1850.

MOST EXPENSIVE BOWLING
IN ONE-DAY INTERNATIONALS

MARTIN SNEDDEN: 12–1–105–2 (New Zealand v England, Oval, 1983)

ASHANTHA DE MEL: 10–0–97–1 (Sri Lanka v West Indies, Karachi, 1987–8)

ARNOLD BLIGNAUT: 9–0–96–2 (Zimbabwe v New Zealand, Bulawayo, 2005)

SANATH JAYASURIYA: 10–0–94–3 (Sri Lanka v Pakistan, Nairobi, 1996–7)

RUDIE VAN VUUREN: 10–0–92–0 (Namibia v Australia, Potchefstroom, 2002–3)

TAPASH BAISYA: 7–0–87–0 (Bangladesh v England, Trent Bridge, 2005)

JAVAGAL SRINATH: 10–0–87–0 (India v Australia, Johannesburg, 2002–3)

WAQAR YOUNIS: 10–0–86–2 (Pakistan v Sri Lanka, Benoni 1997–8)

THIRU KUMARAN: 10–0–86–0 (India v Pakistan, Dhaka, 2000)

TINASHE PANYANGARA: 10–0–86–1 (Zimbabwe v England, Edgbaston, 2004)

Give me a game, where eleven men
Are one for the good of the side,
A duck they will make with a smiling face,
They will field through the day in any place,
Though they finish 'two' – in a two-horse race,
They tried, *and* tried *and* tried!

D. L. A. JEPHSON

A DELICATE PREDICAMENT

BATTING FOR EIGHTEEN OF THE TOWN against the United England XI at Whitehaven in 1881, a fellow named Platt hit a ball in such a way that it deflected down on to his body and lodged in his trousers. The *Penrith Herald* reported:

If he took the ball out he was out for touching the ball while in play; if he stood where he was till a fielder removed it before it touched the ground, he was caught out. After a moment's pause he ran for it, attempting to get out of the boundary and then take the ball out. Pursued by the eleven, he made a circuit of half the ground and was eventually pulled down inside the flags, and in the melee which ensued the ball was shaken clear, and the umpires decided Platt was not out.

[179]

UNLUCKY BREAKS

- Playing for St Peters against Horsted Keynes in 1999, Sussex dentist Rob Hemingway hit a six through his own car windscreen. As he heard the crack, he thought to himself: 'Oops, whose car is that?'

- Twice in the space of three days in 2003, Somerset's Keith Dutch was run out by a deflection at the non-striker's end.

- While wheeling their baby around the boundary during a 1994 club match, Sharon Scott of Kington, Herefordshire, was hit on the head by a six struck by her husband Clive. 'She probably cost me a century,' he complained. 'I went into my shell after that.'

- Gloucestershire batsman Sidney Wells was selected for just one first-class game – against Kent at Bristol in 1927 – but rain forced it to be abandoned without a ball being bowled.

- South Wiltshire captain Rob Wade was ruled out for the season after breaking his collarbone while competing in the fathers' sack race at a school sports day in July 2003.

- Groundsman Brian Lucas had his false teeth crushed by his roller while going about his duties at the Perkins Cricket

Club, Shropshire, in 1997. They had flown out of his mouth when he sneezed.

- The final of a six-a-side festival at Beaconsfield CC, Buckinghamshire, in 1992 was abandoned after a car careered across the pitch, injuring four spectators. It was driven by the club president, eighty-six-year-old Tom Orford, who had come to present the prizes.

- The chief executive of South African cricket, Ali Bacher, failed to make a planned speech in the President's Box at the 1998 Lord's Test because he was trapped in the ladies' toilet. He had wandered in there by mistake to read through his notes.

- Delighted that Harry Makepeace had reached his maiden century, against Sussex at Eastbourne in 1907, Lancashire captain Archie MacLaren immediately declared the innings closed. But during the lunch interval it emerged that the scorers had miscalculated and that Makepeace had only made 99. He had to wait another four years for that elusive hundred.

- On the second evening of the 2003 County Championship match between Hampshire and Gloucestershire, umpire Allan Jones found himself locked overnight in the Rose Bowl ground in Southampton, after sharing fish and chips in a camper van belonging to colleague Alan Whitehead.

THE LANGUAGE OF THE WRIST-SPINNER

Arm ball: ball that goes with the arm.

Bosie: Australian name for a googly, named after its inventor, B. J. T. Bosanquet.

Chinaman (UK): ball bowled by a left-arm wrist-spin bowler that breaks from off to leg when bowled to a right-handed batsman: the stock ball of a left-arm wrist-spinner.

Chinaman (Australia): ball bowled by a left-arm wrist-spinner that breaks from leg to off when bowled to a right-handed batsman: the left-arm wrist-spinner's googly.

Drifter: a slow ball that curves deceptively into or away from the batsman.

Flipper: a relatively slow ball that behaves like a top-spinner. It is usually produced by gripping the ball with the tips of the first and third fingers and 'flipping' it out, so that it emerges from the back or side of the hand with added top spin.

Floater: another term for the drifter.

Googly: ball bowled by a right-arm wrist-spinner that breaks from off to leg: an off-break bowled with a leg-break action.

Leggie (Australia): a bowler of leg-spin, a wrist-spinner.

Slider: a quicker ball delivered from the side of the hand that looks like a leg-break but goes straight on.

Wrong 'un: a ball bowled by a wrist-spinner that turns in the opposite direction from usual – a right-arm bowler's googly or a left-arm bowler's chinaman.

A SPORTING GESTURE

ONE OF THE MOST POPULAR FIXTURES in the Surrey calendar during the 1880s was the annual match between the Coachmen and the Gardeners at Upper Caterham. The Coachmen were captained by a Mr Munday, who wielded an enormous bat, nearly a foot wide, which was painted bright scarlet with pictures of saddles and stirrups on the back. His opposite number, the appropriately named Mr Garlic, boasted a similarly large bat, painted green and with pictures of vegetables, spades and hoes on the reverse. Sportingly, he had made a hole in the middle of his bat to give the bowlers a chance.

DUAL TALENTS

MAJOR JOHN WILSON, who played eleven matches as an amateur for Yorkshire between 1911 and 1913, rode Double Chance to victory in the 1925 Grand National.

TED DEXTER (Sussex and England) played in the English Amateur Golf Championship.

ALAN WALKER was a member of the Australian Rugby League team that toured England in 1947–8 and of the Australian cricket party that went to South Africa in 1949–50.

The legendary W. G. GRACE was the national 440-yard hurdles champion and also represented England at bowls.

CHARLES BULL (Kent and Worcestershire 1929–39) won the English Open men's doubles table tennis title three years in succession from 1928–30.

Former Surrey cricket captain CYRIL WILKINSON won a hockey gold medal for Great Britain at the 1920 Olympics.

Australian Test cricketer VIC RICHARDSON (1924–36) also played baseball for his country.

England cricketer JOHNNY DOUGLAS won a gold medal in middleweight boxing at the 1908 Olympics.

Some years after being junior badminton doubles champion for Somerset, IAN BOTHAM played soccer for Scunthorpe United.

The great CHARLES BURGESS FRY, who played twenty-six Tests for England between 1895 and 1912, held the world long jump record for twenty-one years. He also played football for England in 1901.

ALBERT BROWN, who played one match for Warwickshire in 1932, was beaten in the final of the 1946 English Amateur

Snooker Championships. He twice reached the semi-finals of the World Snooker Championships, in 1950 and 1952.

England spinner GEOFF MILLER (1976–84) represented Derbyshire at table tennis as well as cricket.

Before representing his country at cricket, KEPLER WESSELS was the number one junior tennis player in South Africa in 1973.

In the late nineteenth century, both ALBERT HORNBY and ANDREW STODDART captained England at cricket and rugby union.

England's ANDREW FLINTOFF used to play chess for Lancashire.

REGINALD 'TIP' FOSTER, who played for England 1903–7, is the only man to have captained England at both cricket and soccer.

Yorkshire's NORMAN YARDLEY, who played cricket for England between 1938 and 1950, was six-times North of England squash champion.

PHILIP HORNE, who played Test cricket for New Zealand (1987–90), represented his country at badminton in the Commonwealth Games.

Better known as the hero of England's 1966 World Cup-winning soccer team, GEOFF HURST had previously played one first-class cricket match, for Essex against Lancashire at Liverpool in 1962. He made 0 not out and 0, but took two catches as Essex clinched a 28-run victory. BOBBY MOORE was also a promising schoolboy cricketer and indeed the first time Hurst and Moore played on the same side at any sport was for the Essex schools cricket team.

There was an old man of Bengal
Who purchased a bat and a ball,
Some gloves and some pads –
It was one of his fads –
For he never played cricket at all.

ALFRED AINGER

BOARD OF CONTROL OF 'TEST' MATCHES AT HOME, 1898

(Formed at the request of the Counties, by the MCC)

To consist of the President of the MCC (in the chair), five of its Club Committee, and one representative from each of the ten First-Class Counties that came out at the top of the last season's list.

1. PLAY – In all Test matches play shall begin on the first day at 11.30 a.m.; on the second and third days at 11 a.m. Stumps shall be drawn at 6.30 p.m.

2. UMPIRES – The Umpires shall be appointed by Ballot and shall be paid £10 per match.
3. DISTRIBUTION OF PROFITS – All moneys taken at Stands and

Enclosures at the Test Matches shall, together with the Gate Money in respect thereof, less the Opponents' half of the gross Gate Money and less such expenses as are authorized by the Board, be placed in the hands of the Board for distribution as follows: 30 per cent to the grounds where the matches are played, in equal shares; 10 per cent to the Counties that take part in the Second Division of the County Championship; and 60 per cent to be divided equally among the First-Class Counties and the MCC. But should there be a loss on these matches, such loss shall be divided among the said First and Second-Class Counties and the MCC in the proportion of their respective interests.

4. SELECTION SUB-COMMITTEE – A Sub-Committee of three shall be appointed by the Board to select England teams. Such Sub-Committee shall appoint a Chairman, who shall have a casting vote. The said Committee of three shall in each match select the Captain.

5. TRUSTEES – Two Trustees shall be appointed to whom all payments subject to distribution, as aforesaid, should be made.

6. COLLECTIONS – No collection shall be allowed on any ground during a Test match.

7. EXPENSES – The expenses to be deducted from the gross Gate Money (or in Test matches between Australia and South Africa from the stand money) shall include players (including reserve men), police, umpires, scorers, gate and ground attendants, printing, advertising, luncheons, match balls, and any other items specially sanctioned by the Board.

8. PLAYERS – The remuneration of players shall be £20 per match; of reserve men £10.

9. AMATEURS – Amateurs' expenses to be allowed are railway fares and a sum at the rate of 30s. per diem, not exceeding five days for each match.

10. LUNCHEONS – The amount to be allowed for luncheon will be £10 per diem.

11. SCORERS – Scorers shall be paid £5 per match.

12. ADVERTISING – The sum to be allowed for advertising shall not exceed £30 for each match.
13. TEA INTERVAL – There will be a tea interval at 4.30 p.m. daily during the Test matches, unless at that time 9 wickets of the batting side have fallen, or an interval has occurred since luncheon. In the event of there being no interval, drinks can be sent out on the field at the request of the Captain of the fielding side.
14. NEW BALL – Umpires should inform the batsmen when a new ball is about to be used.

SHORTEST FIRST-CLASS INNINGS

Balls	Total	
53	15	Hampshire v Warwickshire, Edgbaston, 1922
57	26	Leicestershire v Kent, Leicester, 1911
62	16	Warwickshire v Kent, Tonbridge, 1913
67	26	England XI v Australia, Edgbaston, 1884
67	20	Derbyshire v Yorkshire, Sheffield, 1939
69	12	Northamptonshire v Gloucestershire, Gloucester, 1907
70	29	Sussex v Lancashire, Liverpool, 1907
71	19	Matabeleland v Mashonaland, Harare, 2000–1
72	16	MCC v Surrey, Lord's, 1872
72	25	Gloucestershire v Somerset, Cheltenham, 1891

TWIN TWINS

STRANGE THOUGH IT MAY SEEM, South Africa had its own Bedser twins. Alec Bedser, who died in 1981, aged thirty-three, in a Johannesburg road crash, was a right-arm medium-pace bowler who played for Border in the 1971–2 Currie Cup. Like his twin brother Eric (they were named after the English cricketing twins), Alec was an excellent all-round sportsman.

BIG HITTER

UNTIL 1910, six runs were not usually given for a hit unless the ball was dispatched right out of the ground, not just the playing area. This rule was a blow to batsmen like Charles Thornton of Cambridge University, Kent and Middlesex, who hit the ball harder and farther than any player of his day, recording six measured hits of over 150 yards. In 1869 at Canterbury, he launched every ball of a four-ball over well beyond the boundary but earned only four runs for each stroke. Expanding his horizons, Thornton made 107 in 29 hits for the Gentlemen against I Zingari in 1886, sending eight balls clean out of the Scarborough ground. On another occasion – against Merchant Taylors – he lost seven balls.

Wisden CRICKETERS OF THE YEAR

EACH YEAR five players are named by *Wisden Cricketers' Almanack* as cricketers of the year, primarily for their 'influence on the previous English season'. Four players have been honoured as sole recipients – W. G. Grace, John Wisden (posthumously), Plum Warner and Jack Hobbs, the last two selections breaking the general rule that a player may receive the award only once in his career.

1889   Six Great Bowlers of the Year: Johnny Briggs, John Ferris, George Lohmann, Bobby Peel, Charles Turner, Sammy Woods.

1890   Nine Great Batsmen of the Year: Bobby Abel, Billy Barnes, Billy Gunn, Louis Hall, Robert Henderson, Maurice Read, Arthur Shrewsbury, Frank Sugg, Albert Ward.

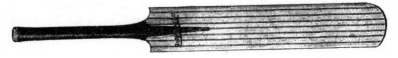

1891 Five Great Wicketkeepers: Jack Blackham, Gregor MacGregor, Dick Pilling, Mordecai Sherwin, Henry Wood.
1892 Five Great Bowlers: William Attewell, J. T. Hearne, Frederick Martin, Arthur Mold, John Sharpe.
1893 Five Batsmen of the Year: Herbie Hewett, Lionel Palairet, Walter Read, Stanley Scott, Andrew Stoddart.
1894 Five All-Round Cricketers: George Giffen, Alec Hearne, Stanley Jackson, Harry Trott, Ted Wainwright.
1895 Five Young Batsmen of the Season: Bill Brockwell, Jack Brown, C. B. Fry, Tom Hayward, Archie MacLaren.
1896 W. G. Grace.
1897 Five Cricketers of the Season: Syd Gregory, Dick Lilley, K.S. Ranjitsinhji, Tom Richardson, Hugh Trumble.
1898 Frederick Bull, Willis Cuttell, Frank Druce, Gilbert Jessop, Jack Mason.
1899 William Lockwood, Wilfred Rhodes, William Storer, Charlie Townsend, Albert Trott.
1900 Joe Darling, Clem Hill, Arthur Jones, Monty Noble, Robert Poore.
1901 Tip Foster, Schofield Haigh, George Hirst, Henry Stratton, Tom Taylor.
1902 Len Braund, Charlie McGahey, Frank Mitchell, Willie Quaife, Johnny Tyldesley.
1903 Warwick Armstrong, Cuthbert Burnup, James Iremonger, James Kelly, Victor Trumper.
1904 Colin Blythe, John Gunn, Albert Knight, Walter Mead, Plum Warner.
1905 Bernard Bosanquet, Ernest Halliwell, James Hallows, Percy Perrin, Reggie Spooner.
1906 David Denton, Walter Lees, George Thompson, Joe Vine, Levi Wright.

1907 Jack Crawford, Arthur Fielder, Ernie Hayes, Kenneth Hutchings, Neville Knox.

1908 Albert Hallam, Reginald Schwarz, Frank Tarrant, Bert Vogler, Tomas Wass.

1909 Lord Hawke and Four Cricketers of the Year: Walter Brearley, Lord Hawke, Jack Hobbs, Alan Marshal, John Newstead.

1910 Warren Bardsley, Sydney Barnes, Douglas Carr, Arthur Day, Vernon Ransford.

1911 Harry Foster, Alfred Hartley, Charlie Llewellyn, Razor Smith, Frank Woolley.

1912 Five Members of the MCC's Team in Australia: Frank Foster, J. W. Hearne, Septimus Kinneir, Phil Mead, Herbert Strudwick.

1913 John Wisden.

1914 Major Booth, George Gunn, Bill Hitch, Albert Relf, Lionel Tennyson.

1915 Johnny Douglas, Percy Fender, Wally Hardinge, Donald Knight, Sydney Smith.

1918 School Bowlers of the Year: Harry Calder, John Firth, Clement Gibson, Gerard Rotherham, Greville Stevens.

1919 Five Public School Cricketers of the Year: Percy Adams, Percy Chapman, Adrian Gore, Lionel Hedges, Norman Partridge.

1920 Five Batsmen of the Year: Andy Ducat, Patsy Hendren, Percy Holmes, Herbert Sutcliffe, Ernest Tyldesley.

1921 Plum Warner.

1922 Hubert Ashton, J. L. Bryan, Jack Gregory, Charlie Macartney, Ted McDonald.

1923 Arthur Carr, Tich Freeman, Charlie Parker, C. A. G. Russell, Andy Sandham.

1924 Arthur Gilligan, Roy Kilner, George Macauley, Cecil Parkin, Maurice Tate.

1925 Bob Catterall, Jack MacBryan, Herbie Taylor, Richard Tyldesley, Dodger Whysall.

1926 Jack Hobbs.

1927 George Geary, Harold Larwood, Jack Mercer, Bert Oldfield, Bill Woodfull.

1928 Roger Blunt, Charlie Hallows, Wally Hammond, Douglas Jardine, Vallance Jupp.

1929 Leslie Ames, George Duckworth, Maurice Leyland, Sam Staples, Jack White.

1930 Ted Bowley, K. S. Duleepsinhji, Tuppy Owen-Smith, Walter Robins, Bob Wyatt.

1931 Donald Bradman, Clarrie Grimmett, Beverley Lyon, Ian Peebles, Maurice Turnbull.

1932 Bill Bowes, Charles Dempster, James Langridge, Nawab of Pataudi Snr, Hedley Verity.

1933 Ewart Astill, Freddie Brown, Alec Kennedy, C. K. Nayudu, Bill Voce.

1934 Fred Bakewell, George Headley, Stan Nichols, Leslie Townsend, Cyril Walters.

1935 Stan McCabe, Bill O'Reilly, George Paine, Bill Ponsford, Jim Smith.

1936 Jock Cameron, Errol Holmes, Bruce Mitchell, Denis Smith, Arthur Wellard.

1937 Charles Barnett, Bill Copson, Alf Gover, Vijay Merchant, Stan Worthington.

1938 Tom Goddard, Joe Hardstaff, Len Hutton, Jim Parks Snr, Eddie Paynter.

1939 Hugh Bartlett, Bill Brown, Denis Compton, Kenneth Farnes, Arthur Wood.

1940 Learie Constantine, Bill Edrich, Walter Keeton, Fred Price, Brian Sellers.

1947 Alec Bedser, Laurie Fishlock, Vinoo Mankad, Peter Smith, Cyril Washbrook.

1948 Martin Donnelly, Alan Melville, Dudley Nourse, Jack Robertson, Norman Yardley.

1949 Lindsay Hassett, Bill Johnston, Ray Lindwall, Arthur Morris, Don Tallon.

1950 Trevor Bailey, Roly Jenkins, John Langridge, Reg Simpson, Bert Sutcliffe.

1951 Godfrey Evans, Sonny Ramadhin, Alf Valentine, Everton Weekes, Frank Worrell.

1952 Bob Appleyard, Tom Dollery, Jim Laker, Peter May, Eric Rowan.

1953 Harold Gimblett, Tom Graveney, David Sheppard, Stuart Surridge, Fred Trueman.

1954 Neil Harvey, Tony Lock, Keith Miller, Johnny Wardle, Willie Watson.

1955 Bruce Dooland, Fazal Mahmood, Eric Hollies, Brian Statham, George Tribe.

1956 Colin Cowdrey, Doug Insole, Jackie McGlew, Hugh Tayfield, Frank Tyson.

1957 Dennis Brookes, Jim Burke, Malcolm Hilton, Gil Langley, Peter Richardson.

1958 Peter Loader, Arthur McIntyre, Collie Smith, Mickey Stewart, Clyde Walcott.

1959 Leslie Jackson, Roy Marshall, Arthur Milton, John Reid, Derek Shackleton.

1960 Ken Barrington, Donald Carr, Ray Illingworth, Geoff Pullar, M. J. K. Smith.

1961 Neil Adcock, Ted Dexter, Roy McLean, Raman Subba Row, Vic Wilson.
1962 Bill Alley, Richie Benaud, Alan Davidson, Bill Lawry, Norman O'Neill.
1963 Don Kenyon, Mushtaq Mohammad, Peter Parfitt, Phil Sharpe, Fred Titmus.
1964 Brian Close, Charlie Griffith, Conrad Hunte, Rohan Kanhai, Gary Sobers.
1965 Geoffrey Boycott, Peter Burge, Jack Flavell, Graham McKenzie, Bobby Simpson.
1966 Colin Bland, John Edrich, Dick Motz, Graeme Pollock, Peter Pollock.
1967 Bob Barber, Basil d'Oliveira, Colin Milburn, John Murray, Seymour Nurse.
1968 Asif Iqbal, Hanif Mohammad, Ken Higgs, Jim Parks Jnr, Nawab of Pataudi Jnr.
1969 Jimmy Binks, David Green, Barry Richards, Derek Underwood, Ossie Wheatley.
1970 Basil Butcher, Alan Knott, Majid Khan, Mike Procter, Don Shepherd.
1971 Jack Bond, Clive Lloyd, Brian Luckhurst, Glenn Turner, Roy Virgin.
1972 Geoff Arnold, Bhagwat Chrandrasekhar, Lance Gibbs, Brian Taylor, Zaheer Abbas.
1973 Greg Chappell, Dennis Lillee, Bob Massie, John Snow, Keith Stackpole.
1974 Keith Boyce, Bevan Congdon, Keith Fletcher, Roy Fredericks, Peter Sainsbury.
1975 Dennis Amiss, Mike Denness, Norman Gifford, Tony Greig, Andy Roberts.
1976 Ian Chappell, Peter Lee, Rick McCosker, David Steele, Bob Woolmer.
1977 Mike Brearley, Gordon Greenidge, Michael Holding, Viv Richards, Bob Taylor.

Thought you might find this
amusing!

Hope you haven't too many
googlies?

love Dad

1978 Ian Botham, Mike Hendrick, Alan Jones, Ken McEwan,
Bob Willis.

1979 David Gower, John Lever, Chris Old, Clive Radley, John
Shepherd.

1980 Joel Garner, Sunil Gavaskar, Graham Gooch, Derek Randall,
Brian Rose.

1981 Kim Hughes, Robin Jackman, Allan Lamb, Clive Rice, Vincent van
der Bijl.

1982 Terry Alderman, Allan Border, Richard Hadlee, Javed Miandad,
Rod Marsh.

1983 Imran Khan, Trevor Jesty, Alvin Kallicharran, Kapil Dev,
Malcolm Marshall.

1984 Mohinder Amarnath, Jeremy Coney, John Emburey, Mike Gatting,
Chris Smith.

1985 Martin Crowe, Larry Gomes, Geoff Humpage, Jack Simmons,
Sidath Wettimuny.

1986 Phil Bainbridge, Richard Ellison, Craig McDermott,
Neal Radford, Tim Robinson.

1987 John Childs, Graeme Hick, Dilip Vengsarkar, Courtney Walsh,
James Whitaker.

1988 Jonathan Agnew, Neil Foster, David Hughes, Peter Roebuck,
Salim Malik.

1989 Kim Barnett, Jeff Dujon, Phil Neale, Franklyn Stephenson,
Steve Waugh.

1990 Jimmy Cook, Dean Jones, Jack Russell, Robin Smith, Mark Taylor.

1991 Mike Atherton, Mohammed Azharuddin, Alan Butcher,
Desmond Haynes, Mark Waugh.

1992 Curtly Ambrose, Phil DeFreitas, Allan Donald, Richie Richardson,
Waqar Younis.

1993 Nigel Briers, Martyn Moxon, Ian Salisbury, Alec Stewart,
Wasim Akram.

1994 David Boon, Ian Healy, Merv Hughes, Shane Warne, Steve Watkin.

1995 Brian Lara, Devon Malcolm, Tim Munton, Steve Rhodes,
Kepler Wessels.

1996 Dominic Cork, Aravinda de Silva, Angus Fraser, Anil Kumble,
Dermot Reeve.
1997 Sanath Jayasuriya, Mushtaq Ahmed, Saeed Anwar, Phil Simmons,
Sachin Tendulkar.
1998 Matthew Elliott, Stuart Law, Glenn McGrath, Matthew Maynard,
Graham Thorpe.
1999 Ian Austin, Darren Gough, Muttiah Muralitharan, Arjuna
Ranatunga, Jonty Rhodes.
2000 Chris Cairns, Rahul Dravid, Lance Klusener, Tom Moody,
Saqlain Mushtaq.
2001 Mark Alleyne, Martin Bicknell, Andrew Caddick, Justin Langer,
Darren Lehmann.
2002 Andy Flower, Adam Gilchrist, Jason Gillespie, V. V. S. Laxman,
Damien Martyn.
2003 Matthew Hayden, Adam Hollioake, Nasser Hussain,
Shaun Pollock, Michael Vaughan.
2004 Chris Adams, Andrew Flintoff, Ian Harvey, Gary Kirsten,
Graeme Smith.
2005 Ashley Giles, Steve Harmison, Robert Key, Andrew Strauss,
Marcus Trescothick.

The merry click of bat against the ball,
The expectant hush, the cheering that proclaims
Skill of the greatest of all English games;
Flutter of flags, the branches of the trees
Swaying beneath the gentle summer breeze;
Nor sweeter music in the world is found
Than that upon an English Cricket ground.

R. RATCLIFFE ELLIS